Br
Kant's *Religion within the*
Boundaries of Mere Reason

David Mills Daniel

scm press

The author and publisher acknowledge material reproduced from
Immanuel Kant, *Religion within the Boundaries of Mere Reason*,
trans. and ed. A. Wood and G. di Giovanni, Cambridge: Cambridge
University Press, revised edition, 1998, ISBN 0521599644.
Reprinted by permission of the Cambridge University Press.
All rights reserved.

British Library Cataloguing in Publication data

A catalogue record for this book is available
from the British Library

978 0 334 04039 2

First published in 2007 by SCM Press
9–17 St Alban's Place,
London N1 0NX

www.scm-canterburypress.co.uk

SCM Press is a division of
SCM-Canterbury Press Ltd

Typeset by Regent Typesetting, London
Printed and bound in Great Britain by
Bookmarque Ltd, Croydon, Surrey

Contents

Contents

Introduction

The SCM *Briefly* series is designed to enable students and general readers to acquire knowledge and understanding of key texts in philosophy, philosophy of religion, theology and ethics. While the series will be especially helpful to those following university and A-level courses in philosophy, ethics and religious studies, it will in fact be of interest to anyone looking for a short guide to the ideas of a particular philosopher or theologian.

Each book in the series takes a piece of work by one philosopher and provides a summary of the original text, which adheres closely to it, and contains direct quotations from it, thus enabling the reader to follow each development in the philosopher's argument(s). Throughout the summary, there are page references to the original philosophical writing, so that the reader has ready access to the primary text. In the Introduction to each book, you will find details of the edition of the philosophical work referred to.

In *Briefly: Kant's Religion within the Boundaries of Mere Reason*, we refer to Immanuel Kant, *Religion within the Boundaries of Mere Reason*, translated and edited by Allen Wood and George di Giovanni, Cambridge: Cambridge University Press, 1998, ISBN 0521599644.

Each *Briefly* begins with an Introduction, followed by a chapter on the Context in which the work was written. Who

Introduction

was this writer? Why was this book written? With Some Issues to Consider, and some Suggestions for Further Reading, this *Briefly* aims to get anyone started in their philosophical investigation. The Detailed Summary of the philosophical work is followed by a concise chapter-by-chapter Overview and an extensive Glossary of terms.

Bold type is used in the Detailed Summary and Overview sections to indicate the first occurrence of words and phrases that appear in the Glossary. The Glossary also contains terms used elsewhere in this *Briefly* guide and other terms that readers may encounter in their study of Kant's *Religion within the Boundaries of Mere Reason*.

Context

Who was Immanuel Kant?

Immanuel Kant, whose ideas on metaphysics, moral philosophy and the philosophy of religion have had such a profound and lasting influence on thinking in all these areas, was born in Konigsberg, East Prussia, in 1724. Although Kant did not come from a wealthy background (his father was a saddler), he was able to become a student at the University of Konigsberg in 1740, where he showed an interest in science and astronomy as well as philosophy. After graduating, Kant worked as a tutor for a number of years, before returning to Konigsberg as a private lecturer at the university in 1755. He was appointed professor of logic and metaphysics in 1770.

In many ways, Kant's life is exactly what we would expect that of a professional philosopher to be. In addition to his teaching responsibilities at the university, where his lectures covered such subjects as physics, geography and anthropology, he devoted himself almost entirely to study, thought and writing. In order to use his time efficiently, he rose before five o'clock in the morning, and followed an unvarying daily routine, allocating fixed periods of time to each activity. His first major work of philosophy, the *Critique of Pure Reason*, was published in 1781. His other books include: *Prolegomena to any Future Metaphysic* (1783), *Groundwork of the Metaphysics of*

Morals (1785), the second edition of the *Critique of Pure Reason* (1787), *Critique of Practical Reason* (1788) and *Religion within the Boundaries of Mere Reason* (1793). Kant died in 1804.

What is *Religion within the Boundaries of Mere Reason*?

In *Religion within the Boundaries of Mere Reason* (referred to below as *Religion*), Kant observes: 'Apart from a good life-conduct, anything which the human being supposes that he can do to become well-pleasing to God is mere religious delusion and counterfeit service of God.' For Kant, the only service God demands from human beings is that they lead morally good lives: they must obey the categorical imperatives of the moral law. True religion is not about trying to please God, through worship and ritual; true religion is the pure religion of reason that teaches people to treat moral laws as divine commands, which it is a sin to transgress. In *Religion* (published, in its entirety, in 1793), Kant discusses a range of Christian theological doctrines and aspects of ecclesiastical organization (he refers to other religions, but is mainly concerned with Christianity), but does so in the context of the deontological system of morality he sets out in the *Groundwork of the Metaphysics of Morals*, and his understanding of the relationship between God and morality, explained in the *Critique of Practical Reason*. It is to be expected, therefore, that he will not take an orthodox Christian view of these subjects.

He reminds his readers (**Prefaces**) that morality is based on the idea that, as rational beings, human beings are free, but also bind themselves by moral laws that they discover through their reason. As these moral laws are obeyed for their own sake, God is not needed to make human beings recognize or perform their duty. However, although morality is independent of religion, because human beings must do what is right for its own sake, God and immortality are what Kant calls postulates of the practical reason (reason when it is concerned with matters of morality): they have to be postulated, in order to make sense of morality. Human beings have an idea of the highest good, in which performance of duty is rewarded by proportionate happiness. Only an all-powerful God can make this highest good possible, while immortality gives human beings the opportunity to achieve moral perfection. Therefore, morality does not depend on religion, but it does lead to it.

Kant (**Prefaces**) also warns that, as human beings diminish even sublime things like religion, it has come to be expressed in forms that depend for their authority on coercive laws, and is also subject to censorship. He urges religious censors to exercise their powers with restraint, and not to impede scholarship and research. However, in 1794, the government of the religiously conservative King Frederick William II of Prussia instructed Kant not to write about religion: an order that he complied with until Frederick William's death in 1797.

Kant accepts (**Part I**) that experience does not support the theory that the world is going from bad to better: it is characterized by moral, as well as physical, evil. But why is this the case when, as free and rational beings, human beings know, through their reason, what the moral law requires of them? It is because they have a propensity to moral evil: there is what Kant calls a 'radical innate evil in human nature'. This sounds like the traditional Christian doctrine of original sin: that, due to the Fall, human beings have inherited a tendency to sin. However, Kant considers it unhelpful to think of this propensity as something that human beings have inherited from their first ancestors, Adam and Eve. Indeed, he warns that use of the word 'nature' is misleading. As the propensity to evil is the determining ground of their power of choice, it relates to human beings as free, moral and morally responsible beings, and so is not physical. If human beings select an evil principle, contrary to the moral law, as the supreme ground of the maxims or rules of conduct they adopt, it is because they have freely chosen to do so.

Here, Kant invokes the distinction between the world of the senses (the phenomenal world), in which human beings, like everything else, are subject to causal laws of nature; and the world of understanding (the noumenal world), in which, as free and rational beings, they are subject to moral laws, grounded on reason, which are independent of nature, and which they impose upon themselves. The exercise of freedom, by which they adopt the supreme ground of their maxims (whether for or against the moral law) occurs in the world of understanding; therefore, they are its authors, and can be held responsible for it.

Kant's distinction between the noumenal and phenomenal worlds complicates his moral philosophy and philosophy of religion. However, it is essential to his approach, because moral responsibility requires freedom to obey, or not to obey, the categorical imperatives of the moral law. In the *Groundwork*, Kant acknowledges that the claim that human beings are free seems to contradict the natural necessity to which they are subject in the phenomenal world, and cannot be proved. But the idea of freedom cannot be given up: it just has to be accepted that there actually is no contradiction between holding that beings who are subject to the laws of nature are also independent of them, and subject to moral laws, given by pure reason. As Kant puts it in *Religion*, human beings must think of themselves as 'already existing free beings', not through creation, but through a 'purely moral necessitation', only possible 'according to laws of freedom'.

Kant explains that even the worst human beings do not repudiate the moral law: their moral predisposition means it imposes itself on them irresistibly and, if no other factors were present, they would make it their supreme maxim, and be morally good. However, to a greater or lesser degree, they allow their physical inclinations to influence their moral choices, and their being good or evil depends on whether these, or the categorical imperatives of the moral law, predominate. Kant accepts that it is impossible to explain exactly how moral evil first entered human beings, and attributing its origin to Satan, as in the Genesis story, does not make it any more understandable. However, by locating the origin of evil in human beings yielding to temptation, the Genesis story indicates that, unlike Satan, they are not fundamentally corrupted and, as they possess a good will, are capable of returning to good.

Human beings are created good, which means that this is their original predisposition and, to regain it, they need to make the moral law the supreme ground of their maxims, and not allow their inclinations to prevail. Kant acknowledges, however, that if they are corrupt in the ground of their maxims, it is difficult to see how they can become good by themselves. Kant allows for the possibility of divine assistance or grace, to help them achieve the necessary revolution in their disposition. However, he is cautious about it. Relying on grace would mean that becoming morally good was not their own doing, but God's. Human beings can only be judged good on the basis of what they achieve themselves and, even if grace is available, Christianity teaches that God will only help people if they make an effort themselves. Anyway, as grace concerns the supernatural, it falls outside the limits of reason. If the moral law commands that human beings ought to be better, they must be capable of doing so. They must make an unremitting effort to be good, and gradually duty for its own sake will become an attitude of mind.

The Bible (**Part II**) teaches that human beings must become holy like God. As it is their duty to do so, it must be possible for them to undergo moral conversion: a complete transformation in their moral disposition. But this would not remove the breaches of the moral law, or sins, they have committed in the past, or prevent their actual deeds being (to some extent) defective. So how can they ever become well-pleasing to God? It is possible because, on the basis of their change of heart, God treats their infinite progress towards obedience to the moral law as a perfected whole: so they can be well-pleasing to God, whenever their lives end. Although they deserved punishment before their conversion, now, as they have a good moral disposition, it would not be appropriate. Again, Kant invokes the distinction between the phenomenal and noumenal worlds. Physically, they are the same human beings, who deserve punishment, but, as intelligible or rational beings they are, in God's eyes, different beings morally. At the same time, human beings cannot be sure that their good disposition will enable them to make unbroken progress in goodness, which prevents them being overconfident. Morality gains from people having to work out their salvation in fear and trembling, and they must be prepared to persevere in this life and the next.

Kant interprets Jesus' life and death in a way that fits in with his system of morality. What God wants to see is humanity in its full moral perfection. As one who, despite temptations, carried out all human duties, and suffered for the world's sake,

Jesus represents the idea of a morally perfect human being. He is a model for humanity, and it is human beings' duty to emulate his moral disposition. But does it matter whether Jesus was a real person? For Kant, this is not the key point. The important thing is that human beings have an idea of one who is able to obey the moral law: what he calls a moral 'prototype'. Such an example does not need to be drawn from experience, as it is present in the reason. However, it can be expressed in terms of Jesus being God's only-begotten Son, and human beings becoming God's children, by adopting his disposition.

Kant explores the issues that arise from belief in the incarnation: that Jesus has a divine origin. While saying that the moral prototype came down from heaven may make Jesus' moral perfection more comprehensible and significant, it has practical disadvantages, as ordinary human beings must seek the prototype they see in him in themselves. Placing Jesus above the frailty of human nature makes it harder to emulate him, or to hold that human beings can reach his level of moral goodness. But what matters is that, when a teacher perfectly exemplifies what he teaches, as Jesus did, and it is everyone's duty to do the same, it must be ascribed to his having a morally pure disposition; and this is valid for all human beings, at all times, and in all places.

Human beings' moral conversion, which they achieve by adopting Jesus' moral disposition, can be interpreted in terms of the traditional Christian doctrines of redemption and atonement. Their new moral disposition, personified as the Son of God, bears their debt of sin for them. The suffering morally renewed human beings must undergo can be seen as a death, suffered once and for all by human beings' representative, and imputed to them by grace, as if already possessed. But the important point is that individuals have the required good disposition, and understand that their only hope of being absolved from the burden of sin and guilt is through a total change of heart and adopting genuine moral principles in their disposition.

As to what they can expect when life ends, they must take their whole lives into account, and not try to excuse themselves on the grounds of human frailty. If they believe that all will be well, they will just hope to get their lives in order by the time they end.

If religion is all about morality, and the moral conversion of the individual, while worship and ritual do not matter, there seems to be no role for the Church. But **(Part III)**, one reason why human beings fail to obey the moral law is that, in society, they corrupt each other's moral dispositions. Therefore, within society or the political state, there needs to be an ethical community, or church, under the direction of God, which is concerned, not with external obedience to coercive laws, but with the morality of human beings' actions, and which will encourage them to obey the moral law.

Kant recognizes that the churches that do, or may, exist in the world fall short of the ideal. He distinguishes between the Church invisible, in which all upright human beings join under direct, yet moral, divine rule, and which is a model for the ones human beings found; and the Church visible, the actual union of human beings, on the basis of this ideal. A true visible Church would show God's moral kingdom on earth, as far as human beings can achieve it; would aim at an ethical union of everyone in the world; and would be free of internal divisions and superstition. Such a universal Church can only be based on the pure religion of reason. It would recognize that obedience to the moral law and good life conduct are the only service God requires, and would treat moral duties as divine commands. However, human beings find it hard to accept that the only service God wants from them is a morally good life, and wish to please God, through performing various services for him, even though they lack moral value. Thus, they gravitate towards a religion of divine service and direct worship of God, based on ecclesiastical rules and rituals, which derive from revelation, rather than towards a purely moral one, based on obedience to the moral law.

While a Church that practises a religion of divine service, based on revelation, is not practising the pure religion of reason, Kant accepts that human beings need something their senses can grasp hold of, to support even the highest concepts. Therefore, pure religious faith needs ecclesiastical faith, and its rules and rituals, to promote and preserve it; but the latter must be interpreted in a way that harmonizes with the universal rules of the former. Revelation is particularly advantageous, when it enables people to arrive more quickly at religious truths, which they could have reached using their reason: they can still use reason to convince themselves of its truth. A holy book can also be a valuable means of preserving the pure religion of reason. For this purpose, exposition of, and scholarly research into, the holy book, should relate its contents to pure moral faith, to enable uneducated church members to understand it, and draw appropriate lessons from it. Kant warns against interpreting scripture on the basis of inner feelings, as they are not reliable guides to the moral law. Such feelings tend to promote undesirable religious enthusiasm, and can undermine respect for moral feeling.

What churches must guard against (**Part IV**) is 'fetishism' or 'priestcraft', which puts observing ecclesiastical rules and rituals, based on revelation, above good life conduct, and which claims that the former are necessary, not as a means to a good moral disposition, but in order to become well-pleasing to God directly. Clergy who teach that ecclesiastical faith alone can save, give the church 'counterfeit service'. They also encourage church members to adopt a security principle in matters of faith: to believe too much rather than too little. In churches dominated by priestcraft, the clergy claim the exclusive right to interpret God's will, and deny church members any moral freedom. In the end, through its influence over people's minds, the Church rules the state as well. Further, the value of ecclesiastical faith for less educated adherents can be overrated. It may offer accessible historical narratives, but the moral law itself has been written in the hearts of even the least educated; and this is what leads them to the pure religion of reason.

What ecclesiastical faith, based on revelation, must do is to try to move ever closer to the pure religion of reason, until it can be set aside as the latter's vehicle. If it does this, it may be regarded as the true faith, even though it is not a moral one, and hopes to please God through actions that lack moral worth. Kant sees the transition to the new order happening gradually, through the permanent revelation of the principle of the pure religion of reason that is occurring in all human beings; and he believes that it will be possible to say that the kingdom of God has entered human beings, even if just the idea of the change from ecclesiastical faith to the pure religion of reason has publicly taken root. Rather optimistically (particularly in a book published during the French revolutionary wars), he sees the present as the best period of church history: the seed of true religious faith, now being sown in Christianity, needs only to be allowed to grow for evidence of an 'invisible Kingdom of God on earth' to begin to develop.

Context

In *Religion*, Kant discusses a wide range of Christian doctrines, beliefs and practices, but from the standpoint of his own philosophical outlook, and in a way that fits them into his system of morality. Generally, he 'shows a strong tendency to strip away, as it were, the historical associations of certain dogmas and to find a meaning which fits in with his own philosophy' (Copleston). This applies to such doctrines as original sin and the atonement, and also to the Trinity. For Kant, the last-mentioned is a helpful way of expressing God's relationship to human beings as moral beings (he is a holy lawgiver, benevolent ruler and just judge), but he warns that regarding the Trinity as what God is in himself goes beyond human understanding; even more crucially, it does not promote human beings' moral improvement. Again, such sacraments and practices as baptism, communion, private prayer and church-going can direct attention to true service of God, but become 'fetish-faith', if not performed in a moral spirit, or if it is believed that taking part in them will please God directly. The communion service, for example, is just a way of emphasizing the idea of the Church as a moral community, and encouraging brotherly love among its members.

Reactions to Kant's treatment of Christianity and its doctrines and practices will vary. More orthodox Christians may consider that Kant simply does not understand what these doctrines and practices really mean, and that his attempt to fit them into his system of morality makes nonsense of them. Others, however, may feel that there is some truth in his view that the doctrines and practices of the Christian churches tend to turn religion, which should (if not exclusively) be concerned with the personal moral improvement of its members, into a form of courtly service. And (even if they do not agree with him), few will deny that there is something grand and inspiring about Kant's conviction that only those who seek to become well-pleasing to God through good life conduct, will give him the veneration he wants.

Some Issues to Consider

- In *Religion within the Boundaries of Mere Reason*, Kant does not take an orthodox Christian view of the theological doctrines and aspects of ecclesiastical organization he discusses.
- Kant holds that what matters to God, and the only service he demands from human beings, is that they lead morally good lives: they must obey the categorical imperatives of the moral law.
- True religion is not about trying to please God, through worship and ritual, but is the pure religion of reason, which teaches people to treat moral laws as divine commands.
- As moral laws are obeyed for their own sake, God is not needed to make human beings recognize or perform their duty.
- Kant regards God and immortality as postulates of the practical reason: they have to be postulated, in order to make sense of morality.
- Human beings have an idea of the highest good, in which performance of duty is rewarded by proportionate happiness: only an all-powerful God can make this highest good possible, while immortality gives human beings the opportunity to achieve moral perfection.
- Kant believes that, although, as free and rational beings, human beings know, through their reason, what the moral law requires of them, moral evil exists, because of the radical innate evil in human nature.

Some Issues to Consider

- Although it sounds like original sin, this propensity to evil should not be thought of as something human beings have inherited from their first ancestors: as the determining ground of their power of choice, it relates to them as free, moral and morally responsible beings.

- If human beings select an evil principle, contrary to the moral law, as the supreme ground of the rules of conduct they adopt, it is because they have freely chosen to do so.

- Kant distinguishes between the world of the senses, in which human beings are subject to causal laws of nature, and the world of understanding, in which, as free and rational beings, they are subject to moral laws, grounded on reason.

- The exercise of freedom, by which they adopt the supreme ground of their maxims (whether for or against the moral law), occurs in the world of understanding.

- Human beings allow their physical inclinations to influence their moral choices, and their being good or evil depends on whether these, or the categorical imperatives of the moral law, predominate.

- Kant accepts the impossibility of explaining how moral evil first entered human beings.

- By identifying evil's origin in human beings succumbing to temptation, the Genesis story indicates that, unlike Satan, they are not fundamentally corrupted, and, as they possess a good will, are capable of returning to good.

- Kant allows for the possibility of divine assistance or grace, to help human beings achieve the necessary revolution in their moral disposition.

- On the basis of their moral conversion and their now having a good disposition, God treats human beings' progress towards obedience to the moral law as a perfected whole:

so they can be well-pleasing to God, whenever their lives end.

- For Kant, Jesus represents the idea of a morally perfect human being: he is a model for humanity, and it is human beings' duty to emulate his moral disposition.
- The idea of Jesus as a moral prototype can be expressed in terms of his being God's only-begotten Son: human beings become God's children, by adopting his disposition.
- Does it matter whether or not Jesus had a divine origin?
- Human beings' moral conversion, which they achieve by adopting Jesus' moral disposition, can be interpreted in terms of the traditional Christian doctrines of redemption and atonement.
- As human beings corrupt each other, there needs to be an ethical community, or Church, within society, which is concerned, not with external obedience to coercive laws, but with the morality of human beings' actions, and which will encourage them to obey the moral law.
- Kant distinguishes between the Church invisible, which is a model for the ones humans found, and the Church visible, the actual union of human beings, on the basis of this ideal.
- A true visible Church would show God's moral kingdom on earth, as far as human beings can achieve it, and would aim at an ethical union of everyone in the world.
- Do human beings find it hard to accept that the only service God wants from them is a morally good life, and gravitate towards a religion of divine service and direct worship of God?
- Ecclesiastical faith is useful as a means of promoting and preserving the pure religion of reason.
- Ecclesiastical faith should move ever closer to the pure

religion of reason, until it can be set aside as its vehicle.

- Scripture should not be interpreted on the basis of inner feelings, which are not a reliable means of recognizing that laws are moral.
- Kant deplores fetishism or priestcraft, which puts observing ecclesiastical rules and rituals, based on revelation, above good life conduct, and which claims that the former are necessary, not as a means to a good moral disposition, but in order to become well-pleasing to God directly.
- Is Kant too harsh in what he says about some Christian churches and their priests or ministers?

Suggestions for Further Reading

Immanuel Kant, *Critique of Practical Reason*, ed. V. Politis, London: Everyman, 1993.

Immanuel Kant, *Critique of Pure Reason*, ed. M. Gregor, Cambridge: Cambridge University Press, 1997.

Immanuel Kant, *Groundwork of the Metaphysics of Morals*, ed. M. Gregor, Cambridge: Cambridge University Press, 1997.

Immanuel Kant, *Religion within the Boundaries of Mere Reason*, eds A. Wood and G. di Giovanni, Cambridge: Cambridge University Press, 1998.

Immanuel Kant, *Prolegomena to any Future Metaphysic*, ed. B. Logan, London: Routledge, 1996.

E. Cassirer, *Kant's Life and Thought*, trans. J. Haden, New Haven, CT: Yale University Press, 1981.

F. Copleston, *A History of Philosophy*, vol. 6, Part II (Kant), New York, NY: Image Books, 1964.

P. Guyer (ed.), *The Cambridge Companion to Kant*, Cambridge: Cambridge University Press, 1992.

M. Kuehn, *Kant: A Biography*, Cambridge: Cambridge University Press, 1998.

G. E. Michaelson, *Kant and the Problem of God*, Oxford and Malden MA: Blackwell, 1999.

G. Thomson, *On Kant*, revised edition, Belmont, CA: Wadsworth/Thomson Learning, 2002.

Detailed Summary of Kant's *Religion within the Boundaries of Mere Reason*

Preface to the first edition (pp. 33–9)

Its being based on the conception of human beings as 'free', but also binding themselves through their '**reason** to **unconditional laws**', means **morality** requires neither a superior being to get them to recognize their **duty**, nor any '**incentive** other than the **law** itself' to carry it out (p. 33). Thus, morality does not require religion. It is 'self-sufficient by virtue of pure **practical reason**', and needs 'no **end** either in order to recognize what duty is or to impel its performance' (p. 33). For example, I do not need to have an end I might achieve to tell the truth in a 'court of justice', or to be honest, and return another's goods, which are in my safekeeping, when they are reclaimed (pp. 33–4). One who needs such an end is 'already contemptible' (p. 34).

However, although morality requires no end that comes before the '**determination of the will**', it may need one, not as the '**ground of its maxims**', but as a '**necessary consequence**' of conforming to them (p. 34). Although morality does not need 'an end for right conduct', the answer to the question, '*What is then the result of this right conduct of ours*', cannot be a '**matter of indifference to reason**' (p. 34). We have the idea of a '**highest**

good in the world', in which **happiness is proportioned to the observance of duty**; and this assumes 'a **higher, moral, most holy, and omnipotent being'**, who can make it possible (p. 34). The idea of thinking that 'all our doings and nondoings' have 'some sort of **ultimate end'** meets a 'natural need', but this idea 'rises out of morality': it is 'not its foundation' (p. 34). Thus, morality 'inevitably leads to religion', and the idea of a 'mighty moral lawgiver', 'whose will' can and 'ought to be the ultimate human end' (pp. 35–6).

And, just as morality recognizes that the 'holiness of its law' should be respected, religion recognizes an 'object of *worship*' in its 'highest cause' (p. 36). But, human beings diminish even '**sublime'** things, and what can be properly 'venerated', only when this is done freely, has to be adapted to 'forms', whose 'authority' depends on 'coercive laws'; and, as it is open to 'public criticism', subject to '**censorship'** (p. 36).

The command to obey 'authority' is a 'moral one', which can be 'extended to religion', but it is important to see this in a wider context than obeying a particular 'regulation' (pp. 36–7). A '**theologian'**, who passes judgement on books, can be just a '**divine'**, whose sole concern is with the well-being of '**souls'**, or also a university academic, concerned with the interests of scholarship (p. 37). The latter concern should have priority: we do not want a situation in which a '**biblical theologian'** sets out to 'humble' the '**sciences'**, through control of all areas of intellectual enquiry (p. 37). Further, as well as 'biblical theology', there is '**philosophical theology'**, which must be given free rein, provided it stays within the 'boundaries of mere reason', and does not try to change the 'public doctrines' of the former or, if it '*borrows*' material from biblical theology, does not use it inappropriately (pp. 37–8). In fact, it would be a good idea, if biblical theologians completed their academic education with a course in the 'pure *philosophical* doctrine of religion', to prepare them for the kind of issues **philosophers** raise (pp. 38–9). They should be willing to listen to what philosophers have to say, even if they ultimately disagree with it.

These four essays examine how religion relates to a human nature that comprises both good and **evil** '**dispositions**' (p. 39).

Preface to the second edition (pp. 40–1)

Nothing is 'altered in this edition' (p. 40). As far as its title is concerned, '*revelation*' can include the '**pure** *religion of reason*', but, 'conversely', this is not the case with the 'historical' in revelation; and the philosopher, as a 'teacher of reason', from 'principles *a priori*', must stay within his own 'circle' (p. 40). This makes it possible to begin with an 'alleged revelation', and, 'abstracting from the pure religion of reason', to hold parts of it, as a '*historical* system', up to 'moral concepts', and see if it leads back to the 'same *pure rational system* of religion' (p. 40). If it does, we can say that 'reason and Scripture' are not only compatible, but also form a 'unity', so that following one will mean encountering the other (p. 40).

I have not been able to examine all the 'judgments' made about this book, but (in response to one opinion), I must stress that only 'common morality', not a critique of the 'practical' or '**theoretical reason**', is needed to understand it (p. 41).

Königsberg, 26 January 1794

Detailed Summary

Part I: Concerning the indwelling of the evil principle alongside the good, or Of the radical evil in human nature (pp. 45–73)

It is an old 'complaint' that the world now 'lieth in evil': that, having begun with a '**Golden Age**' of 'happiness', it is now characterized by '**physical**' and '**moral evil**', with 'destruction' close at hand (p. 45). The opposite view is that it is going from 'bad to better' (p. 45). But, if our concern is with '*moral* good or evil', as opposed to mere 'growth in civilization', 'experience' does not support the latter theory, which seems to be an 'optimistic' view of '**moralists**' like **Seneca** and **Rousseau**, to encourage development of the 'seed of goodness' within us (pp. 45–6). But, we could say that, just as human beings are 'sound of body by nature', they are, too, 'of soul' (p. 46).

Perhaps, the truth lies between these two extremes: that human beings are 'partly good, partly evil' (p. 46). We must recognize that we cannot judge a human being '**evil**', just because he does evil things: those 'contrary to law' (p. 46). Experience enables us to identify 'unlawful actions', even ones that are 'consciously' so, but not to 'observe maxims', so we are unable to base such judgements 'reliably' on it (p. 46). We judge a human being evil, because we can '**infer** *a priori*', from one or more 'consciously evil actions', the 'presence' of an 'underlying evil maxim', and thus, 'a common ground' of 'all particular morally evil maxims' (p. 46).

The word '*nature*' may shock some; it seems to contradict the terms '*morally* good or *morally* evil', and suggest the 'opposite' of 'grounds of action' arising from '*freedom*' (p. 46). But, it refers only to the 'subjective ground' of the 'exercise of the human being's freedom in general', which precedes every action, and which, if a human being is to be held responsible for his choices, must always be a 'deed of freedom' (p. 46).

Part I: Concerning the indwelling of the evil principle

The 'good or evil' in him could not be called '"moral"', if the whole 'exercise of freedom' could be accounted for by 'natural causes' (pp. 46-7). Any 'ground of evil' cannot 'lie' in some 'natural impulse', which determines choice, but in a 'maxim' that the '**power of choice** itself produces for the exercise of its freedom' (pp. 46-7). To say a particular human being is good or evil 'by nature', just means that he has within him a 'first ground' (impenetrable to others) for 'adoption of good or evil' maxims, and that, through his maxims, he expresses the '**character of his species**' (p. 47). These two 'characters' are '*innate*' in a human being, but nature should not be blamed, if is it evil, or praised, if it is good: he 'is alone its author' (p. 47). As the 'first ground' of the 'adoption of our maxims', in relation to the '**moral law**', cannot come from 'experience', the good or evil in a human being is 'innate' only '*in the sense*' that it is 'posited as the ground antecedent to every use of freedom given in experience' (p. 47). It is present in him at 'birth', but is not caused by it (p. 47).

Remark (pp. 47-50)

The **proposition**, '*The human being is* (by nature) *either morally good or morally evil*', is '**disjunctive**'. It could be, as 'experience' suggests, that a 'middle position' is more tenable, and human beings are both good and evil (p. 47). The danger of this, for '**ethics**', is that the 'morally intermediate' can mean 'all maxims' losing their 'determination and stability' (pp. 47-8). This is the position of '*rigorists*', who hold that the 'peculiar' characteristic of 'freedom of the power of choice' is that nothing can determine it 'to action', unless the '*human being has incorporated it into his maxim*': that is, made it a '**universal** rule', by which he 'wills to conduct himself'; '*latitudinarians*' hold the opposite view (pp. 48–9). However, the 'moral law' is an 'incentive in the judgment of reason', so one who adopts it as his 'maxim' is *'morally* good'; and, to be 'good in one part' is to have 'incorporated' the moral law into one's maxim (p. 49). In contrast, one who 'incorporates', in his maxim, 'deviation from the moral law', is an 'evil human being', whose 'disposition' towards the moral law is 'never indifferent' (p. 49).

Describing these two dispositions as 'innate' does not mean a human being is not the 'author' of his particular disposition, but that he has not 'earned' it 'in time', and so has always had it (p. 50). It applies to his 'entire use of freedom universally', and must have been freely 'adopted' (p. 50). But, we do not know 'the cause of this adoption', so we describe it as an attribute that the 'power of choice' has 'by nature', although it is 'grounded in freedom' (p. 50). Whether, when we say a particular human being is 'good or evil by nature', we are saying it of the 'whole species', can only be shown, if it becomes clear, 'from **anthropological research**', that one of the two 'characters' applies to all human beings without exception (p. 50).

I Concerning the original predisposition to good in human nature (pp. 50–2)

We can put this under 'three headings': (1) the human being's **'predisposition'** to *'animality'*, as a *'living being'*; (2) to his *'humanity'*, as both a living and *'rational* **being'**; (3) to his *'personality'*, as a rational and *'responsible* being' (p. 50).

1 The first comes under 'merely *mechanical* self-love' (that does not require 'reason'), and has three parts: for 'self-preservation'; for the 'propagation' and 'preservation' of 'the species'; and for 'community' with other humans. On to

these, such 'vices' as *'lust and wild lawlessness'* towards others can be 'grafted' (p. 51).

2   The second comes under 'self-love which is physical', but requires reason, as it judges whether or not one is happy, 'in comparison with others' (p. 51). From it comes the 'inclination *to gain worth in the opinion of others'* which, through 'anxiety' that others are seeking 'ascendancy', can lead to an 'unjust desire' to gain 'superiority' over them (p. 51). From the *'jealousy* and *rivalry'*, thus created, can arise 'hostility to all whom we consider alien to us' (p. 51). These 'vices' do not 'issue from' nature 'as their root', as they are a way of gaining 'security' against the general 'competitiveness' that nature intended only as 'an incentive to **culture**', and which does not rule out '**reciprocal love**' (p. 51). They can be called 'vices of *culture'*, and, in the forms of *'envy'* and *'ingratitude'*, can be *'diabolical'* (p. 51).

3   The third is '**susceptibility** to simple respect for the moral law within us', which is an 'incentive of the power of choice', and which is 'possible only because the free power of choice incorporates moral feeling into its maxim' (p. 52). Such a 'power of choice' is 'good character', which can only be 'acquired'; but, for 'its possibility', 'our nature' must have a 'predisposition onto which nothing evil can be grafted' (p. 52). Indeed, the 'idea of the moral law', and 'respect' for it, are 'personality itself'; and 'incorporating this incentive into our maxims' is 'an addition' to it (p. 52). As to the 'conditions' that make these 'predispositions' possible, the first does not have 'reason at its root'; the second is 'rooted' in a 'practical' reason, but is 'subservient to other incentives'; only the third is rooted in '**reason legislating unconditionally**' (p. 52).

The three predispositions are not only (by not resisting the 'moral law') negatively *'good'*, but are also (by demanding 'compliance with it') *'to the good'* (p. 52). They are *'original'*, as they belong to the 'possibility of human nature' (p. 52). The first two can be used 'inappropriately', but not removed. The only predispositions we are concerned with here are those relating 'immediately' to 'the faculty of **desire**' and the 'exercise of the power of choice' (p. 52).

II   Concerning the propensity to evil in human nature (pp. 52–5)

We are talking of human beings' *'natural* **propensity**' to genuine, 'i.e. moral evil', which belongs to them 'universally', and which they can be thought of as having *'brought'* on themselves (p. 53). There are three 'grades' of this propensity to evil: human nature's *'frailty'* ('general weakness' in complying with the maxims of the moral law); *'impurity'* ('incentives', other than those of the moral law, being needed to choose 'what duty requires'); and *'depravity'* (subordinating the 'incentives of the moral law to others (not moral ones)') (pp. 53–4). It is 'woven into human nature', and so exists in even 'the best' human beings (p. 54). As concerns 'agreement of actions' with the moral law, there is no difference between a human being 'of good morals' and a 'morally good' one; but the former complies only with its *'letter'*, while the latter 'observes' its *'spirit'*, as this is 'sufficient incentive' (p. 54). When determination of the 'power of choice to *lawful* actions' depends on other 'incentives', such as 'ambition' or even 'sympathy', it is 'purely accidental' if 'actions agree with the law': the maxim, by the 'goodness' of which the person's **moral worth** must be measured, is 'contrary to law', and so, despite good actions, he is 'evil' (p. 54).

The propensity to evil is not 'physical', as it originates 'from freedom', and relates to 'a human's power of choice as moral being' (p. 54). Only a 'deed', for which we are responsible, can be morally evil, but a propensity is a 'determining ground of the power of choice' that '*precedes every deed*', and so is not yet one (p. 55). However, there are two senses of 'deed': the 'use of freedom', by which the '**supreme maxim**', whether for or against the moral law, is 'adopted in the power of choice', and the actions that result from its adoption (p. 55). The propensity to evil is a deed in the first sense, and so the 'formal ground' of 'every deed contrary to law' (p. 55). While the second is '**empirical**, given in time', the first is an '**intelligible**' one, '**cognizable** through reason alone' (p. 55). It is 'innate', as it cannot be 'eradicated': for that, the 'supreme maxim' would need to be 'good', but in 'this propensity', it has 'been assumed to be evil' (p. 55). Although it is 'our own deed', we do not know why 'evil has corrupted the very highest maxim in us' (p. 55).

III   The human being is by nature evil (pp. 55–61)

Saying human beings are evil means they are 'conscious of the moral law', but have 'incorporated' deviations from it into their maxims (p. 55). We cannot infer this from the 'concept' of human beings 'in general', but know it 'through experience' (p. 56). To be 'morally evil', and something human beings can be 'held accountable for', 'this propensity' cannot be a 'natural predisposition' (p. 56). It comes about through our 'own fault': we can call it a '*radical* innate *evil* in human nature', although 'not any the less brought upon us by ourselves' (p. 56). We do not need '**formal proof**' that this 'corrupt propensity' exists, given the evidence of terrible 'human *deeds*' (p. 56). This is the case both when human beings are in a '*state of nature*' and in a 'civilized state', as, for example, when we hate someone 'to whom we are indebted' (pp. 56–7). Then we have the 'state of constant war' between nations, and universal derision of hopes of 'perpetual peace' and good international relations (p. 57).

The 'ground of this evil' cannot lie in the human being's '**sensuous** nature' and 'natural **inclinations**', as it relates to him as a 'freely acting being' (pp. 57–8). He must be 'capable' of being held 'guilty' of it; otherwise, it would eliminate the 'incentives originating in freedom', and make the 'human a purely *animal* being' (p. 58). But, it cannot be located in '*corruption* of the morally legislative reason', as if reason could eliminate 'within itself the dignity of the law itself' (p. 58). It would be a 'contradiction' to think of ourselves as 'freely acting' beings, but not subject to the moral law, which is the only law 'commensurate' to such beings; an 'absolutely evil will' would create a '*diabolical* being' (p. 58).

Even the 'worst' human being does not, 'whatever his maxims', 'repudiate the moral law', by 'revoking obedience to it' (p. 58). His 'moral predisposition' means it 'imposes itself on him irresistibly' and, were there no other factors, he would make it his 'supreme maxim', and be 'morally good' (p. 58). But, there are 'incentives of his sensuous nature', which he incorporates into his maxim (pp. 58–9). Now, if he treated these as '*sufficient*' to determine his choice, without heeding the moral law, he would be 'morally evil' (p. 59). What happens is, he 'incorporates both into the same maxim', so whether he is 'good or evil' depends on which is subordinated to the other (p. 59). Human beings are evil, because they make the 'incentives of self-love and their inclinations' the condition of complying with the moral law, when the latter should be the 'sole incentive' (p. 59). However, even when a human being's maxim is 'contrary to the moral order', his actions can still comply with the moral law, as when someone is honest, in order to avoid the 'anxiety' of telling lies: here, the 'empirical character' is good, but the 'intelligible' one, evil (p. 59).

This propensity is 'morally evil' (it must 'ultimately be sought in a free power of choice'); '*radical*' (it 'corrupts the ground of all maxims'); and it cannot be '*extirpated* through human forces' (it assumes the 'subjective supreme ground of all maxims' to be 'corrupted'): although it must be possible to '*overcome* this evil', as it is found 'in the human being as acting freely' (p. 59). It is not '*malice*', which would be incorporating evil in one's maxims '*qua evil*', but '*perversity*', which is called '*evil*', due to its results (p. 60). It derives from human 'frailty': human nature is too weak to abide by its 'adopted principles', and dishonest in not properly identifying the true 'incentives' of actions, 'in accordance with the **moral guide**' (p. 60).

Human beings' '*innate* **guilt**', which can be spotted in their first 'exercise of freedom', but which originates from it, and for which they are accountable, can, in the stages of 'frailty and impurity', be considered 'unintentional' (p. 60). But the third stage is 'deliberate guilt', when the 'human heart' deceives itself as to whether its 'disposition' is evil, provided its actions do not produce evil (p. 60). Such 'dishonesty' impedes development of a 'genuine moral disposition'; it can be called 'unworthiness', and stems from the 'radical evil of human nature' (pp. 60–1). It has been said, 'Every man has his price, for which he sells himself' but, if this is so, St **Paul** is right: 'there is none righteous (in the spirit of the law), no, not one' (p. 61).

IV Concerning the origin of evil in human nature (pp. 61–5)

If an effect is related to a cause, 'according to the laws of freedom', as is the case with 'moral evil', it is 'bound' to it, not 'in time but merely in the representation of reason' (pp. 61–2). To try to find the 'temporal origin of free actions as free', as if they were 'natural effects', is a 'contradiction' (p. 62). But, however moral evil originated in human beings, the most unsatisfactory way of 'representing its spread' is to think of it as inherited from 'our first parents' (p. 62). When we look for the 'rational origin' of an 'evil action', we must think of it as if the agent had 'fallen into it directly from the state of innocence', and accept that whatever the 'natural causes' he was subject to, the action was free and not 'determined' by any of them: an action must always be regarded as an *'original* exercise' of the 'power of choice' (pp. 62–3). A person may have been evil until the moment of a 'free action', but his 'duty to better himself' is a present one, which he is able to perform, and he is 'accountable', if he fails to do so (p. 63). It is not possible to investigate such a deed's 'origin in time', only its 'origin in reason'; and then attempt to explain why there is this propensity to evil (p. 63).

Appropriately, the Bible represents evil as beginning, not from a 'fundamental propensity to it', which would prevent it being the 'result' of freedom, but from *'sin'*: 'transgression of the moral law as *divine command*' (p. 63). The moral law, as suited a being, 'tempted by inclinations', is depicted as a *'prohibition'* (p. 63). The human being started to question it, making his obedience 'conditional', and subordinating the 'incentive of the law' to 'other aims' (pp. 63–4). He included this in the 'maxim of action', and 'sin came to be'; and this is what we do 'daily' (pp. 63–4). Thus, '"in **Adam** we have all sinned"', and 'still sin': however, in us an 'innate propensity' to sin is presupposed, whereas, in Adam, 'innocence is pre-supposed with respect to time' (p. 64). But, although we wish to discover the 'origin in time' of a 'moral character for which we are to be held accountable' (and the Genesis story makes allowance for this weakness), we must not do so (p. 64).

The important point of the story is that human beings' evil propensity or sin was not 'co-created' with them; rather, the 'first human being', in full 'control' of his reason, chose to sin (p. 64). Thus, sin was 'generated directly from innocence', and 'remains inexplicable' (p. 64). Evil can have 'originated only from moral evil' but, as our 'original predisposition', which only we 'could have corrupted', if we are to be held responsible for this, is 'to the good', it is impossible to explain how 'moral evil could first have come in us' (p. 64). The Bible addresses this 'incomprehensibility' through a 'historical narrative', which locates the '*first* beginning of all evil' in a '*spirit*'; but, then, why was it there (p. 65)? This does not remove the in-comprehensibility, but, by showing human beings as having succumbed to '*temptation*', it portrays them, in contrast to the spirit, as not 'corrupted *fundamentally*', and, as they possess a 'good will', capable of returning 'to the good' (p. 65).

General Remark concerning the restoration to its power of the original predisposition to the good (pp. 65–73)

To say human beings are 'created good' means this is their 'original *predisposition*'; that they have been created 'for the *good*'; and that they determine whether they will be 'good or evil', by whether or not they incorporate the 'incentives con-tained in that predisposition' into their 'maxims' (p. 65). If this requires 'supernatural cooperation', they must make them-selves 'antecedently worthy' of it, and '*accept*' it (pp. 65–6).

Detailed Summary

A tree, 'originally good' in its predisposition, produces 'bad fruits', but is capable of returning to good (p. 66). Despite our 'fall', we are aware of the 'command that we *ought* to become better', so a 'germ of goodness' remains in us (p. 66).

Recovery of our 'original disposition to good' means we regain the '*purity* of the law', which becomes the 'supreme ground of all our maxims' and not subordinate to 'inclinations' (p. 67). Habitual compliance with duty is '***virtue***' in its '*empirical character*'; it is developed gradually, through 'reformation of conduct', so that a 'propensity to vice' becomes the opposite; but it does not require a '*change of heart*' (p. 67). To be 'virtuous' in its 'intelligible character', and to need 'no other incentive to recognize a duty', except duty itself, can only be achieved by a '*revolution* in the disposition': a 'transition to the maxim of holiness of disposition' (pp. 67–8).

However, if the human being is 'corrupt' in the 'very ground of his maxims', how can he, by himself, 'become a good human being' (p. 68)? In this way: if he 'reverses the supreme ground of his maxims', he will become a 'subject receptive to the good'; but only through 'incessant' toil will he '*progress* from bad to better' and become a 'good human being' (p. 68). For God, who knows the 'intelligible ground of the heart', this is the same as 'actually being a good human being'; but, for the human being, it is a constant 'striving' for gradual reformation of the propensity to evil (p. 68). 'Moral education' must start with transforming the 'attitude of mind', and there is no 'better way' to cultivate 'predisposition to the good' than to observe 'the *example* of good people', and then examine the 'incentives' that 'actually' underlie their actions (pp. 68–9). Little by little, '*duty* merely for itself' becomes an 'attitude of mind' (p. 69). What we can only 'wonder' at, is our 'original moral predisposition' which, despite our being 'dependent on nature', places us 'far above it' (p. 69). This pre-disposition announces a 'divine origin', fortifies our minds for the 'sacrifices' that 'respect for duty' may require, and inspires us to restore 'the original ethical order' among our incentives (pp. 69–70).

It seems impossible to reconcile belief that the human being can restore his good predisposition, through his 'own effort', with the belief that he is innately corrupt (p. 70). And it is not comprehensible to us. However, if the moral law 'commands that we *ought* to be better human beings', we must be '*capable*' of being so (p. 70). The 'transformation' of the 'disposition of an evil human being' into that of a good one is taken to lie in the new and 'unchangeable' 'supreme inner ground' of the adoption of all his maxims (his 'new heart'), which will now be in accord with 'ethical law' (p. 71). He will not himself be able to obtain evidence of this, because he cannot penetrate the 'depths' of his heart, but, he can hope that his own efforts will take him in the right 'direction': he 'ought to become a good human being', and can only be 'judged *morally* good' on the basis of what he achieves himself (p. 71).

Religions of 'mere cult' can mislead here, and teach that God will remit the human being's '**debts**', and make him '**eternally happy**', without his needing to become better, or make him so, if he just asks (p. 71). But, Christianity, a '**moral religion**', teaches that only if he exerts himself will what lies outside his power be 'made good' by help 'from above': although he will not know in what this help consists (pp. 71–2).

This 'General Remark' is the first of four about subjects touching on 'religion within the boundaries of pure reason': (1) 'Of **Effects of Grace**'; (2) '**Miracles**'; (3) '**Mysteries**'; and (4) '**Means of Grace**' (p. 72). Reason, aware that it is powerless to 'satisfy its moral needs', turns to 'extravagant ideas', which it cannot 'incorporate' into its 'maxims of thought and action' (p. 72). They are treated as matters of '*reflective*' faith: reason recognizes the dishonesty of calling them '*knowledge*' (p. 72). In religion, these ideas have their respective 'disadvantages': (1) '*enthusiasm*'; (2) '*superstition*'; (3) '*illumination*, the delusion of the initiates'; (4) '*thaumaturgy*': 'attempts at influencing the supernatural (means of grace)' (p. 72). About the '*effects of grace*', specifically, it is an issue that falls outside the 'limits' of reason, as does any 'supernatural' question; such effects cannot be made '*theoretically* cognizable', as our 'concept of cause and effect' cannot go beyond 'objects of experience' (p. 72). Further, expecting an 'effect of grace' would mean the 'morally good' was 'not of our doing', but that of 'another being' (p. 73).

Part II: Concerning the battle of the good against the evil principle for dominion over the human being (pp. 77–102)

To become a 'morally good human being', it is not enough just to let the 'germ of the good' develop; the 'opposing cause of evil' must also be 'combatted' (p. 77). The **Stoics** understood that there was such an 'enemy', but were wrong to think it lay in the 'natural inclinations' which, '*in themselves*', are '*good*', and just need to be controlled, through '*prudence*', and 'harmonized into a whole called happiness' (pp. 77–8). The 'evil' principle, present in the 'human moral battle', is not omitting to 'struggle' with inclinations; it is not recognizing that this is not just a 'natural error', but is 'itself contrary to duty', and that its cause lies, not in the inclinations, but in 'that which determines the power of choice as free power of choice' (p. 78).

It is not surprising that 'an **apostle**' depicts this 'corrupter of basic principles' as 'evil spirits', and tells us that it is against these, not 'flesh and blood (the natural inclinations)', that we 'have to wrestle' (p. 79).

Section 1   *Concerning the rightful claim of the good principle to dominion over the human being (pp. 79–93)*

A   *The personified idea of the good principle (pp. 79–81)*

The only thing that can make a world the 'object of divine decree and the end of **creation**' is humanity in its '*full moral perfection*' (p. 79). The idea of such a human being '**proceeds from God's being**'; he is his '**only-begotten Son', without whom 'nothing that is made would exist**' (p. 80). We become 'children of God' by adopting his 'dispositions', and it is our duty to '*elevate* ourselves to this ideal of moral perfection' (p. 80). But, as this 'idea' has 'established itself' in us, rather than our being 'its authors', it is preferable to say that this '*prototype*' came down 'from heaven' (p. 80). It is more comprehensible that the '**Son of God**' should take up humanity, by '*descending* to it', than that human beings, '*evil* by nature', should renounce it, and elevate themselves to the '**ideal of holiness**' (p. 80). To promote the 'world's greatest good', 'this God-like human being' subjected himself to its 'sufferings', but human beings are never 'free of guilt', even when they have adopted the 'very same disposition' (p. 80). We can only conceive of 'moral perfection' as the 'idea' of a human being, prepared, despite 'temptation', to carry out 'all human duties'; to 'spread goodness' about him through 'teaching and example'; and to undergo suffering, including '**ignominious death**', for the sake of the world and 'his enemies' (p. 80). It is only through '*practical faith in this Son of God*', that human beings can hope to be 'pleasing to God' (p. 80).

B   *The objective reality of this idea (pp. 81–4)*

This idea has 'complete reality within itself', being resident in our '**morally-legislative reason**' (p. 81). We '*ought*', and so we must '*be able*', to 'conform to it' (p. 81). The moral law 'commands unconditionally' and, even though no one had ever been able to obey it unconditionally, the 'objective necessity' of such a person would be 'self-evident' (p. 81). An example of such a '**model**' from 'experience' is not required, as the idea of one thus 'morally pleasing to God' is 'present' in 'our reason'; and anyone who demands 'miracles' as '**credentials**' proves his own 'lack of faith in virtue': and only faith in the idea 'in our reason' has 'moral worth' (p. 81). Indeed, '**outer experience**' cannot provide an 'example adequate to the idea', as it does not show the 'inwardness of the disposition', but only permits 'inference to it' (pp. 81–2).

If a human being had come down 'from heaven', at a particular point in history, led an exemplary life, 'well-pleasing to God', and accomplished 'great moral good', through a 'revolution' in human beings, we would have no reason to think he was anything other than a 'naturally begotten' human, who felt obliged 'to exhibit such an example in himself' (p. 82). We might accept his supernatural origin, but it would have no 'practical' advantage, since we, though ordinary human beings, must seek the 'prototype' we see in him in ourselves (p. 82). Indeed, placing this '**Holy One**' above the 'frailty of human nature' makes it harder for us to emulate him (p. 82). The 'distance' between the 'divine human being' and ordinary ones would be so 'infinitely great' that he could not serve as an *'example'* (p. 82). People may say that, with a **'perfectly holy will'**, they could resist 'every temptation to evil', while assurance of partaking in the 'eternal glory of the **Kingdom of Heaven'** would enable them to endure 'all sorrows', and 'willingly' accept an 'ignominious death' (p. 82). True, we would feel 'love and thankfulness' to one who had relinquished his 'eminence and **blessedness** from eternity', to save 'unworthy individuals' from '**damnation**', and living by 'so perfect a rule of morality' would be a 'valid' **precept** for us to follow; but he himself could not be put forward as 'proof' that we could achieve and practise so 'pure and exalted a moral goodness' (p. 83).

But this 'divinely disposed teacher' would be 'speaking only of the disposition which he makes the rule of his actions' (pp. 83–4). As he cannot make it 'visible' to others, he does so 'externally', through 'teachings and actions' (p. 84). When a teacher is an 'irreproachable example' of what he teaches, and this is 'a duty for everyone', it must be ascribed to his having the 'purest' disposition; and this disposition is 'perfectly valid' for all humans, 'at all times, and in all worlds' (p. 84). It will be a 'righteousness which is not our own', in that ours would have to 'come into existence' in conduct that was 'unfailingly in accord with that disposition' (p. 84). But, an '**appropriation**' of it for the 'sake of our own' must be possible, provided ours is 'associated with' that of the 'prototype': although all this is hard to understand (p. 84).

C   *Difficulties that stand in the way of the reality of this idea, and their solution (pp. 84–93)*

In the conduct of our lives, we are asked to be 'holy' as our **'Father in heaven'** is', for this is the 'ideal of the Son of God'

(p. 84). However, there is a great 'distance' between the 'good-ness' we should bring about in ourselves, and the 'evil' from which we begin (p. 84). Yet, our 'moral constitution' should agree with this holiness, which must be present in our dis-position as the 'germ from which all good is to be developed', and which 'proceeds' from our adopting a 'holy principle' as our 'supreme maxim' (p. 84). And, as it is 'a duty', such a 'change of heart' must be possible (p. 84). But how can the 'disposition count for the deed itself', when the latter is always 'defective' (p. 84)? Our concept of cause and effect is limited to '**temporal conditions**' so, while we see ourselves gradually progressing towards 'something better', our actual deeds are still 'inadequate to a **holy law**' (pp. 84–5). But our underlying disposition 'transcends the **senses**', and God treats our 'infi-nite' progress towards 'conformity to the law' as a 'perfected whole' (p. 85). Thus, we can be '*generally* well-pleasing to God', whenever our lives end (p. 85).

What about our '*moral happiness*' (p. 85)? How can we be sure of the 'reality and *constancy*' of a disposition that will always advance 'in goodness', and never waver (p. 85). If we could be certain of its '*unchangeableness*', and that we would constantly seek 'the **Kingdom of God**', it would be 'equivalent' to our knowing that we already possessed it, in that we would be able to assure ourselves that we shall receive all that 'relates to **physical happiness**' (p. 85). We could say '(**God's**) **Spirit**' will give '**witness to our spirit**', so anyone with the required 'pure' disposition would feel that he would not return to love of evil (p. 85). However, feelings of 'presumed supernatural origin' are unsatisfactory; it is easy to be 'deceived' in what 'promotes a good opinion of oneself', while morality gains through one's having to '"work out one's **salvation** with *fear* **and** *trembling*"' (p. 85). But, without 'confidence in the disposition', we will be discouraged from persisting (pp. 86). What we can do is observe the steady improvement in our lives, since adopting the good 'principles', and from this 'infer' improvement in our disposition, while gaining some assurance that we will 'persevere' in our 'present course', both in this life and (if one 'awaits' us) the next; and so get 'ever closer' to the '**goal of perfection**' (p. 86). However, one whose life goes from 'bad to worse' will have to conclude that 'corruption' is 'rooted in his disposition' (p. 86). The first is a 'glimpse' of a *'boundless* future' that is 'desirable and happy'; the second, of 'a *misery*' that is equally *'boundless'* (p. 86). And, although we do not have to believe 'an eternity of good or evil' definitely will be our 'lot', these glimpses will reassure one section 'of humanity', while spurring others to 'break with evil' (p. 86). The 'good and pure disposition of which we are conscious' gives assurance of its own 'perseverance', and is our 'Comforter (**Paraclete**)' when we doubt it (pp. 87–8). As we are inferring the unchangeableness of our disposition from its effects on the 'conduct of our life', complete 'certainty' is neither possible, nor 'morally beneficial' (p. 88). When close to death, we may feel 'hopelessness' about 'our moral state', but given the 'obscurity' of things that 'transcend the limits of this life', our 'human nature' stops this becoming 'wild despair' (p. 88).

Another 'difficulty' is that we *'started from evil'*, a 'debt' it is 'impossible' to 'wipe out' (p. 88). Good conduct cannot build up 'a surplus', because one's duty is always to do 'all the good' one can (p. 89). Indeed, this debt, which 'precedes whatever good' we may do, is what is meant by '**radical** evil'; it is a 'debt of sins' that 'only the culprit, not the innocent can bear' (p. 89). Moral evil, which is 'called sin when the law is taken *as divine command*', involves 'an *infinity*' of breaches of the law, and so 'an *infinity* of guilt' (p. 89). Thus, every human being should 'expect *infinite* punishment and exclusion from the Kingdom of God' (p. 89). The 'difficulty' is resolved thus. Prior to his '**conversion**', the human being certainly deserved punishment, but now his 'good disposition' has the 'upper hand'; he has become a '"new man"', and punishment cannot be deemed appropriate (p. 89). But, '**Supreme Justice**' cannot permit one, deserving of punishment, not to be, so it must be regarded as 'adequately executed' in the conversion (pp. 89–90). This is both an 'exit from evil' and an 'entry into goodness', but, as evil can only be set aside, through adopting the 'good disposition', it is one, not 'two moral acts' (p. 90). Exchanging the 'corrupted disposition' for 'the good' is itself a 'sacrifice', as, in the 'disposition of the Son of God', the 'new human being' will have to endure all 'life's ills'; and this is 'fitting *punishment*' for the 'old human being' (p. 90). '*Physically*', this is the same human being, who deserves 'punishment', but, as an '**intelligible being**', he is now, in the 'divine' judge's eyes, '*morally* another being' (p. 90). And this pure new disposition, the 'idea' of which we can '**personify**' as the 'Son of God' bears, as '*vicarious substitute*', his 'debt of sin' for him (pp. 90–1). On this interpretation, the 'suffering' which the 'new human being' must undergo, 'throughout his life', is shown as a 'death suffered once and for all' by human beings' 'representative' (p. 91). This is the 'surplus over **merit** from works', sought previously, and which is 'imputed to us *by grace*'; although we are going through a process of becoming 'well-pleasing to God', this is 'imputed to us' as if 'already possessed' (p. 91). Does this idea of the human being's '*justification*' have any 'practical use' (p. 92)? The important point is that the individual has the 'required good disposition', which brings 'comfort and hope' to those 'conscious of it' in themselves (p. 92). The human being must understand that his only hope of being absolved from the burden of 'guilt' is through a total change of heart': no '**expiations**' or '**invocations**' can be a substitute (p. 92).

What can a human being 'expect *at the end of his life*' (p. 95)? Although he may be convinced his 'disposition' has improved, he must take his previous one, and the extent of his improvement, into account (p. 92). He must judge '*his whole life*', not just the final, and best, part of it (p. 93). What 'verdict' will he 'pronounce upon his future life', on the basis of his 'conduct so far' (p. 93)? Addressed to the 'judge' within himself, this question will elicit a 'stern judgment', because 'reason' cannot be bribed (p. 93). But, human beings tend to invoke the excuse of 'human frailty', or try to ward off judgement by pointless 'self-inflicted torments' or 'professions of faith' (p. 93). If they believe '"All is well that ends well"', they will not sacrifice too many of 'life's pleasures', but just hope to get their lives in order by the time they end (p. 93).

Section 2 Concerning the evil principle's rightful claim to dominion over the human being, and the struggle of the two principles with one another (pp. 94–8)

The 'Holy Scriptures' portray this 'moral relation' as a story, in which two 'opposed' principles, 'outside the human being', test their powers on him (p. 94). According to the **Book of Genesis**, he is made 'proprietor' of the earth's 'goods' under God, 'his **Creator**', but there is also an '**evil being**' who, though originally good, has rebelled against 'his master' and lost his heavenly 'estate' (p. 94). He persuades our 'first parents' to rebel against God, and become 'dependent on him'; thus, he establishes himself as '**prince of this world**' (p. 94). It might seem surprising that God did not wipe out this '**Kingdom of Evil**', but his dealings with 'rational beings' are in keeping with the 'principle of their freedom' (p. 94). So, Adam's 'descendants' pursue 'this world's goods', and ignore the 'abyss of perdition' awaiting them (p. 94).

The 'good principle' did keep a foothold in the world, through the establishment of the '*Jewish* **theocracy**', dedicated to its 'veneration' (pp. 94–5). But, as its laws were only partly 'ethical', and were obeyed only through 'external compulsion', while the question of the 'inferiority of the moral disposition' was not considered, it did little harm to the 'realm of darkness' (p. 95). Then, 'suddenly', there appeared 'among these very people' one, whose 'wisdom' indicated he had come 'from heaven' (p. 95). He presented himself as a '**true human being**', but also 'of heavenly origin', and not 'implicated' in the 'bargain' human beings had made with the 'evil principle' (p. 95).

The 'prince of this world' felt his 'sovereignty' would be threatened, if other human beings listened to this person, and adopted his 'disposition' (p. 96). When he failed to tempt 'this stranger' to join him, he caused him (without, in any way, diminishing his 'steadfastness') to be persecuted, and eventually to endure 'ignominious death' (p. 96). The 'physical result' of this 'combat' was the 'good principle' being the 'worsted party' (p. 96). However, the '*principles*' of good and evil have power in the 'realm' of freedom, not nature: as a 'manifestation of the good principle', the 'master's' death gave an example of 'humanity in its moral perfection' for others to follow (pp. 96–7). In fact, this 'good principle' has been present, in some 'invisible way', from the 'beginning of the human race'; but, by 'exemplifying' it, this particular 'human being' threw open the 'doors of freedom' to all those choosing to 'die to everything that holds them fettered to earthly life to the detriment of morality' (p. 97).

The 'moral outcome' of this 'conflict' is not defeat of the 'evil principle', but, as it reveals to them another 'moral dominion', where they can find 'freedom' and a place of 'protection for their morality', its power to control them, 'against their will', is ended (p. 97). But, as the 'evil principle' remains 'prince of this world', adherents of the 'good principle' must expect 'persecutions' (p. 97). When we strip away the narrative's **mystical cover**, its 'meaning' is clear: there can be no 'salvation for human beings', unless they adopt 'genuine moral principles in their disposition' (p. 97). It is **self-incurred** perversity', or 'wickedness', that stops them, and this will only be conquered by the 'idea of the moral good', together with awareness that it is part of 'our original predisposition' and that, if we fully embrace it, the 'powers of evil' have nothing to deploy against it (p. 98). What we must not do is follow superstitious practices; 'this good' has no 'distinguishing trait', other than a 'well-ordered conduct of life' (p. 98). It is our duty to find in 'Scriptures' a 'meaning' in accord with the *most holy* teachings of reason' (p. 98).

General Remark (pp. 98–102)

Establishment of a 'moral religion' that treats 'human duties as divine commands' means there is no need for 'faith in miracles', and we display 'moral unbelief', if we require them to endorse 'duty's precepts' (p. 98). But, when a religion, based on the 'moral disposition', replaces one of **cult and observances**', it fits in with the way the human mind works that it is accompanied by miracles, as these appeal to followers of the old one, encouraging them to view it as a **prefiguration**' of the new (p. 98). And, even when the 'true religion' can 'hold its own on rational grounds', there is no need to challenge those miracles, which can be honoured for helping to gain acceptance for teachings, 'whose **authentication rests on a document indelibly retained in every soul**', and needs 'no miracle' (p. 99). But it must be understood that believing in 'historical reports' of them will not make us 'well-pleasing to God' (p. 99).

There are 'rational human beings', who accept miracles '*in theory*', but do not allow this belief to affect 'practical matters' (p. 99). Sensible governments have not disputed '*ancient*' miracles, but have not recognized '*new*' ones, which can be socially disruptive (p. 99–100). What are miracles? They are 'events', the 'causes' of which are 'unknown to us', and which divide into '*theistic* or *demonic*' (such as 'evil spirits') (p. 100). With the former, we think of God as the world's 'creator and ruler', according to both the 'order of nature' and the 'moral order' (p. 100). But, if God allows 'nature to deviate from such laws', we cannot fathom the basis on which he does so, except for the '*general moral* law' that he always does what is good (p. 100). Demonic miracles are 'irreconcilable' with reason, for, while we can evaluate alleged examples of theistic ones, by the 'negative criterion' that, if they breach morality, they cannot be, this test is not applicable to the former (p. 100).

Practically, miracles cannot affect how we use our 'reason' (p. 101). Whatever a judge may profess in church, he ignores the 'delinquent's' claim of being tempted by the devil (p. 101). Although human 'moral improvement' may be affected by 'heavenly influences', we have no criterion by which to identify them, or distinguish them from 'natural ones' (p. 101). Thus, we must attend to the 'precept of reason', and behave as if all moral 'improvement' results from our own efforts (p. 101).

Part III: The victory of the good over the evil principle, and the founding of a kingdom of God on earth (pp. 105–47)

The most the 'morally well-disposed' human being, directed by the 'good principle', can achieve in his battle with the 'evil principle' is to be free of its *'dominion'*, and 'live for righteousness' (p. 105). The human being's 'perilous state' is his own 'fault': how can he 'extricate' himself from it (p. 105)? He is easily persuaded that the danger comes, not from his own 'raw nature', but from being with others (p. 105). This is when such 'malignant inclinations' as 'envy' and 'addiction to power' attack him: human beings 'corrupt each other's moral disposition', making 'one another evil' (p. 105). And, indeed, the good principle's 'victory' over the 'evil one' can only be achieved by establishing and promoting 'a society in accordance with, and for the sake of, the laws of virtue', which can be a 'rallying point' for lovers of 'good' (p. 106). This *'ethical community'* can exist within the 'political' one, and can be called an *'ethical state'*, that is, a *'kingdom* of virtue (of the good principle)' (p. 106).

Division 1   Philosophical representation of the victory of the good principle in the founding of a kingdom of God on earth (pp. 106–29)

I   Concerning the ethical state of nature (pp. 106–8)

In a political or *'juridico-civil'* state, human beings are subject to **'coercive laws'**; in an *'ethico-civil'* one to *'laws of virtue'* only (p. 106). The members of an 'existing political community' are in an *'ethical state of nature'*, but may wish to have the 'dispositions to virtue' that coercion cannot provide (p. 107). Indeed, coercion would prevent the creation of a community 'directed to ethical ends', by subverting its 'ends'; the citizens of the political community must be 'totally free' to enter, or not enter, 'an ethical union' (p. 107).

II   The human being ought to leave the ethical state of nature in order to become a member of an ethical community (pp. 108–9)

Human beings 'mutually corrupt' each other's 'moral pre-disposition' and, like *'instruments of evil'*, cause each other to stray from the 'common goal of goodness', putting each other at risk of 'falling' under the 'dominion' of evil (p. 108). Just as they should refrain from 'injustice' and 'war', to enter a **'politico-civil state'**, they should do so, too, with the 'ethical state of nature', in which the 'principles of virtue' battle with an 'inner immorality' (p. 108). This is a duty the 'human race' has to itself, as rational beings' 'common end' is to promote 'the highest good as a good common to all' (pp. 108–9). But the individual cannot do this alone; it requires a 'union' of 'well-disposed human beings', to build a 'universal republic based on the laws of virtue' (p. 109). But, we do not know whether this is in 'our power'; a 'higher moral being' may be needed, to unite the 'forces of single individuals' (p. 109).

III   The concept of an ethical community is the concept of a people of God under ethical laws (pp. 109–10)

A *'juridical'* community is not an *'ethical'* one, as the latter's laws concern what is *'internal'*, the *'morality of actions'*, not, as with 'public laws', their external *'legality'* (p. 109). 'Ethical laws' cannot derive '*originally*' from the 'will' of a 'superior' lawgiver, as this would make the duty to obey them, not a matter of 'free virtue', but an 'enforceable legal duty' (pp. 109–10). In an ethical community, the 'supreme lawgiver' must be one in relation to whom ethical duties can be 'represented' as 'his commands', and who can 'penetrate' into each person's disposition (p. 110). This is God, the world's 'moral ruler', and an ethical community is only 'conceivable' as a '*people of God*', acting '*in accordance with the laws of virtue*' (p. 110). There are theocracies, in which God is 'lawgiver', but the laws concern the 'legality', not the 'morality' of actions (p. 110). An ethical community is one in which 'lawgiving' is 'internal, a republic under laws of virtue' (p. 110). Opposed to this '*people* of God' is a '*band* under the evil principle' (p. 110). It is in evil's interest to stop the 'other union', although, of course, this principle also 'resides in our very self' (p. 110).

IV The idea of a people of God cannot be realized (by a human organization) except in the form of a church (pp. 111–12)

Human beings cannot fully realize the 'idea' of an ethical community; the 'form' of one is the 'best' to be hoped for (p. 111). Only God can establish a 'people of God', but each person must behave as if everything 'depended on him' (p. 111). What must be done to make the 'kingdom of God come' (p. 111)? An ethical community that is not an 'object of a possible experience' (in which all 'upright human beings' join under 'direct yet moral' divine rule, and which 'serves' as 'the archetype' for one humans found) is 'called the *church invisible*'; the '*church visible*' is the 'actual union of human beings', in accord with 'this ideal' (p. 111). Most members form a *'congregation'* under 'teachers', who run 'the affairs of the church's invisible supreme head' (p. 111). The 'true (visible) church' shows God's '(moral) kingdom' on 'earth', as far as it is achievable 'through human beings' (p. 111). Its 'marks' are: **(1)** *'Universality'*, being based on 'principles that necessarily lead to universal union', so no '**sectarian schisms**' (pp. 111–12); **(2)** *'purity'*, in having only moral 'incentives' and no 'superstition' (p. 112); **(3)** *'Relation'*, under the 'principle of *freedom*' in members' 'internal' relations and the church's relation to the 'political power' (p. 112); **(4)** *'modality*, the *unchangeableness* of its *constitution'*: there may be modifications to administrative regulations, but it must have clear 'principles', and lay down rules of 'instruction', 'once and for all', in a 'book of laws', not 'changeable' and contradictory '**creeds**' (p. 112). An ethical community's 'constitution' is not like a political one. (p. 112) It is more like that of a 'household', with an 'invisible moral father', whose son, in 'blood relation' with the family members, makes known the father's will to them; and they 'honor the father in him', and enter a 'free, universal and enduring union of hearts' (p. 112).

V   The constitution of each and every church always proceeds from some historical (revealed) faith, which we can call ecclesiastical faith; and this is best founded on a holy scripture (pp. 112–17)

A 'universal church' can only be based on *'pure religious faith'* that is 'rational'; the 'influence' of a '**historical faith**' is limited to the 'credibility' of the 'facts' on which it is based (pp. 112–13). But, human beings find it hard to accept that all God requires of them is 'steadfast zeal in the conduct of a morally good life' (p. 113). They feel they should be performing some '*service*' to God, however 'morally indifferent' the actions involved (p. 113). Thy do not see that, in discharging their 'duties toward human beings', they are '*constantly in the service of God*', who can be served in no 'other way' (p. 113). God is thought to be like a 'great lord of this world', who wants honour and praise from his 'subjects'. The result is a **religion of *divine service***', rather than a 'purely moral' one (p. 113).

In religion, as concerns our duties, God is the 'lawgiver to be honored universally'; and either he commands through '*merely **statutory***' **laws** or '*purely moral*' ones (p. 113). With the latter, we can recognize God's will, through our 'reason': indeed, the idea of God arises from 'consciousness of these laws', and so we can think of 'only *one* religion' that is 'purely moral', as of '*only one*' God (pp. 113–14). But 'statutory laws' can be known only through 'revelation', which would be a '*historical* and not a *purely **rational faith***' (p. 114). Even if there are 'divine statutory laws', 'pure *moral* legislation' is the 'condition of all true religion'; the former can only be 'means' of promoting it, as they cannot 'reach' all human beings, and so do not 'bind' them (p. 114). Those seeking to become 'well-pleasing' to God, through 'good life conduct', will be the ones giving him the 'veneration' he wants (p. 114).

Reason, though, seems unable to answer the question of how people should honour God 'in *a church*'; this seems to require 'statutory legislation', derived from revelation (p. 114). This 'moral community' of different human beings needs a '*public* form of obligation', based on 'divine statutory laws' that are regarded as a duty, giving rise to '"ecclesiastical"', as opposed to 'pure religious faith' (p. 114). However, we should allow for it being 'God's will' that we should establish 'such a community' ourselves (p. 114). When it is set up, it is 'presumptuous' to think its laws are immediately 'divine and *statutory*', though 'arrogant' to deny that a 'special divine **dispensation**' underlies its organization, especially if it is in 'harmony with moral religion' (p. 115). But, whatever is the case, there is evidence of a 'human propensity' for a *'religion of divine service'*, based on revelation, and direct 'veneration of the supreme being', as opposed to obedience to 'his commands already prescribed to us through reason' (p. 115). Human beings do not consider the 'form' of any *'public* institution' for promoting the 'moral [content] of religion' as 'necessary' in itself, but only as a means of serving God, through 'festivities, professions of faith in revealed laws', and so on (p. 115). Although 'morally indifferent', these are thought to please God, because done 'just for his sake'; and so, in shaping human beings into an ethical community, '**ecclesiastical faith** naturally precedes **pure religious faith**' (p. 115).

If a 'statutory *ecclesiastical faith*' is not added to the 'pure faith of religion' as a means of promoting it, the latter's 'preservation' cannot be achieved 'through *tradition*', but only 'through *scripture*' (pp. 115–16). A 'holy book' receives the 'greatest respect', and 'history proves' that a scripture-based faith can withstand even the greatest 'political revolutions' (p. 116). It is 'fortunate' when the book, in addition to 'statutes legislating faith', also contains the 'purest moral doctrine of religion', and can 'command an authority equal to that of a revelation' (p. 116).

There is only *'one* (true) *religion'*, and this can be found in 'various churches' that differ in their 'kinds of faith' (p. 116). Thus, it is better to talk of different faiths (Christian, Jewish, and so on) than different religions, as 'ordinary' people will misinterpret the latter, and think it refers to their own 'ecclesiastical faith', not the religion within that 'depends on moral dispositions' (pp. 116–17). And, indeed, what history has called 'religious struggles' have just been 'squabbles over ecclesiastical faiths' (p. 117). When a church claims to be 'the only universal one', those choosing not to belong, or who reject 'nonessentials' of faith, are called unbelievers, or '*erring*' believers, while those who reject something 'essential' are denounced as **heretics**, and 'expelled'; the 'correctness' in 'matters of ecclesiastical faith', claimed by a church's 'teachers', is called '*orthodoxy*' (p. 117).

VI Ecclesiastical faith has the pure faith of religion for its supreme interpreter (pp. 118–22)

Although, by basing itself on a 'faith of revelation', a church loses any 'legitimate claim to universality', human beings' 'natural need' for something '*the senses can hold on to*', to support even the 'highest concepts', makes 'historical ecclesiastical faith' necessary (p. 118). This '**empirical faith**' must be interpreted in a way that 'harmonizes' with the 'universal practical rules' of a 'pure religion of reason', so it works towards discharging 'all human duties as divine commands' (p. 118). The 'thoughtful teachers' of all 'types of faith' have aligned their 'content' with the 'universal principles of moral faith' (p. 119). Thus, Greek and Roman '**moral philosophers**' presented 'even the coarsest **polytheism**', which is found in the 'legends' about their gods, as a 'symbolic representation' of the attributes of 'one divine being'; and there are 'highly forced interpretations' in Judaism and Christianity (p. 119). Such interpretations do not make nonsense of the 'popular' faith's 'literal meaning', as the 'predisposition to moral religion' preceded it, and lies 'hidden in human reason'; so, the popular faith's 'poetic fabrications' contain some element of 'the character of their **supersensible** origin' (p. 119). There is no 'dishonesty', provided it is not claimed that the 'meaning' given to the popular faith's 'symbols', is exactly as originally intended; but we should remember that the 'final purpose' of the latter is to 'make better human beings' (p. 119). Scriptural '**exegesis**' should relate its contents to the 'rules and incentives of pure moral faith', as this is the 'true religion in each ecclesiastical faith' (p. 120).

Below the 'interpreter of Scripture' comes the *'scriptural scholar'*, whose role is to establish the 'historical credibility' of the 'holy Scripture', on which a church's 'authority' is based (p. 120). This may only amount to establishing that nothing in its 'origin' prevents its being accepted as 'divine revelation', but this satisfies those who find 'special strengthening of their moral faith' in the idea of 'revealed Scripture' (p. 120). Also important is *'exposition'*, so that 'unlearned' church members can understand the scripture's 'meaning', and draw appropriate lessons from it (p. 120). The interpreters and scholars are the 'trustees' of holy scripture, whose work must not be interfered with by the state; its duty is only to ensure there are sufficient scholars and 'morally good' people to 'govern' the Church (pp. 120–1).

There is another contender for the 'office' of scriptural interpreter: 'inner *feeling*' (p. 121). Undeniably, the 'impulse to good actions' the individual feels, after studying scripture, must convince him of its 'divine nature': this is the 'effect of the moral law', which should be regarded as a 'divine command' (p. 121). But we cannot base our recognition that laws are 'moral', or our conviction of 'direct divine influence', on 'a feeling', as this is 'private' and could have 'more than one cause' (p. 121). Doing so would invite 'every kind of enthusiasm', and might undermine the status of the 'moral feeling', by linking it with 'fanciful ones' (p. 121). Scripture is the only 'norm of ecclesiastical faith', and the '*religion of reason* and *scholarship*' its only 'expositor'; but only the first is 'valid for the whole world' (p. 121). In the end, 'ecclesiastical faith' is just 'faith in scholars', making it all the more important that these allow 'public scrutiny' and debate of their interpretations (pp. 121–2).

VII   The gradual transition of ecclesiastical faith towards the exclusive dominion of pure religious faith is the coming of the kingdom of God (pp. 122–9)

A true church's 'distinguishing mark' is '*universality*' (p. 122). A 'historical faith' has 'validity' just for those familiar with its 'history'; only the 'pure faith of religion', based on reason, can be 'recognized as necessary' and the '*true* church' (p. 122). But, if the former can draw ever nearer to the latter, until it can be set aside as its 'vehicle', it may be regarded as the '*true* one'; at first, just a '**church** *militant*', it can become the 'all-unifying church *triumphant*' (p. 122). The faith of those '(worthy of) eternal happiness' is a '*saving*' one, but the 'faith of a religion of service' is '*slavish*' (p. 122). It is not a moral one, based on 'pure dispositions of the heart', but hopes to 'please God' by actions that lack 'moral worth', and which, as they do not require a 'morally good disposition', an 'evil' person can do (pp. 122–3). A saving faith has 'two conditions for its hope of blessedness': the 'lawful undoing (before a judge) of actions done' (which it cannot accomplish itself) and 'conversion to a new life conformable to its duty' (which it can) (p. 123). The former is faith in '**redemption**'; the latter, in becoming 'well-pleasing to God', through 'good conduct'; and they are connected 'necessarily' (p. 123). But we only see the connection by assuming, either that faith in our '**absolution**' **from** '**debt**' will bring forth 'good life conduct', or that the 'active disposition' of the second will bring forth 'faith in that absolution' (p. 123). We need to resolve this 'remarkable **antinomy of human reason**', in order to decide whether historical faith is actually a crucial part of 'saving faith over and above the pure religious one', or whether it will ultimately 'pass over' into the latter (p. 123).

1 If 'satisfaction' has been made for human 'sins' and, if availing himself of it was just a matter of '*faith*', every sinner would swiftly do so (p. 123). But how could any 'rational human being', knowing he deserves punishment, accept that, simply by believing that satisfaction has been made, his 'guilt' has been taken away, and that 'good life conduct' will flow from this (p. 123). It is only 'possible', if the faith is thought of as 'heavenly instilled', and that 'reason' does not need to 'account' for it further (pp. 123–4). If he cannot do this, a person must think of it as 'conditional', and regard 'improvement of his life conduct' as having to occur, prior to any hope of benefiting from 'favor from on high' (p. 123). But, if historical knowledge of the 'favor' is part of ecclesiastical faith, but 'improved life conduct' part of 'pure moral faith', the latter '*must take precedence over the ecclesiastical*' (p. 124).

2 However, if the human being is 'corrupt by nature', and still in the 'power of the evil principle', how can he believe himself capable of becoming a '"new man"', 'well-pleasing to God' (p. 124)? If he cannot see himself as 'reconciled' through the 'satisfaction' made for him, and thus, for the first time, able to lead a 'new life', faith in 'merit' that is 'not his own' must come before 'striving for good works', contradicting the 'previous proposition' (p. 124). This problem cannot be 'resolved theoretically' but, in practical terms, we must start

from 'what we ought to do in order to become worthy of it' (p. 124). Accepting 'faith in a **vicarious satisfaction**' is the only way to make 'removal of sin *comprehensible*' theoretically, but the 'command' that the human being does his duty is 'unconditional'; he must start with improving his life as the 'supreme condition under which alone a saving faith can occur' (pp. 124–5).

It is sometimes said the first 'principle' leads to '**ritual *superstition***', which can 'reconcile a criminal life conduct with religion', whereas the second can result in '*naturalistic unbelief*', uniting 'antagonism to all revelation' with 'exemplary conduct of life' (p. 125). Faith in the 'prototype of a humanity well-pleasing to God (the Son of God)' refers, '*in itself*', to a 'moral idea of reason', which is both a 'guideline' and an 'incentive', and it does not matter whether we start from it as '*rational* faith' or the 'principle of a good life conduct' (p. 125). On the other hand, faith in the prototype, '*according to its appearance* (faith in the **God-man**)', is not, as '*empirical* (historical) faith', the same as the 'principle of a good life conduct', which must be 'totally rational', and starting from it does seem 'quite different'; so, there seems to be a 'contradiction' (p. 125). However, the 'true object of the saving faith' is not that in the 'God-man', which can be 'cognized through experience', but in the 'prototype lying in our reason'; and such faith is the same as 'the principle of a good life conduct' (p. 125). Thus, there are not two different principles here, but 'one and the same practical idea' (pp. 125-6). One 'represents' the prototype as 'situated in God', the other 'in us'; but both represent the 'prototype as the standard measure of our life conduct' (p. 126). But making 'historical faith in the actuality of an appearance' the 'condition' of 'saving faith' would create two conflicting principles, one 'empirical', the other 'rational' (p. 126). Holding that there was once a human being, whose 'holiness and merit' are such that all can hope to be 'blessed in the course of a good life', just through 'this faith', is very different from holding that we must do our utmost to lead a life 'well-pleasing to God', so that we can believe that his love for us will make up, given our 'honest intention', for our 'deficiency in action' (p. 126). All religions have experienced this clash between the two 'principles of faith' (p. 126). While priests have bemoaned 'neglect' of forms of service, established to 'reconcile the people' with God, 'moralists' have deplored the 'decay of morals', and held unexacting 'remission of sin' responsible for it (p. 126). And this is the danger of believing that an 'inexhaustible fund' is available for 'repayment of debts', and all we have to do is 'help ourselves' (p. 126). Yet again, if it is believed that this faith, though considered simply 'historical', is capable of 'radically' improving human beings, just by their holding on to it, it would have to be seen as 'inspired directly by heaven', and everything, including the human 'moral constitution', would be 'reduced to an unconditional decree of God' (pp. 126–7).

'Holy tradition' and its 'observances' have served a purpose but, as the human being matures, they become a 'fetter' (p. 127). Our 'moral predisposition' requires that religion be 'gradually' set free of all historical 'statutes', so that, finally, the 'pure faith of religion will rule over all' (p. 127). This will end the 'distinction between *laity* and *clergy*': there will be 'equality', due to the freedom which results from each individual obeying the law he has 'prescribed for himself', but which is seen as the 'will of the world ruler', 'revealed' through reason (pp. 127). He will bring all human beings together under a 'common government', for which the 'visible church' has been a preparation (p. 128). This 'transition to the new order' will happen, not through 'external revolution', with all its devastating consequences, but through 'gradual reform', arising from the permanent 'revelation' of the 'principle of the pure religion of reason' that is occurring 'within all human beings' (p. 128). And we can say the 'Kingdom of God is come into us', even if just the 'principle' of the 'transition from ecclesiastical faith to the universal religion of reason' has publicly taken root (p. 128). For, in it lies the 'basis for a continual approximation to the ultimate perfection': 'truth and goodness', once 'made public', are bound to flourish, due to their 'natural affinity' with rational beings' 'moral predisposition' (p. 128). Unobserved, the 'good principle' creates its 'kingdom' in human beings, leading to the conquest of evil and 'eternal peace' (p. 129).

Division 2   Historical representation of the gradual establishment of the dominion of the good principle on earth (pp. 129–39)

Being based on 'pure moral faith', 'religion' is not a 'public condition', so the individual can only become aware of his 'advances' in faith 'for himself'; a 'universal historical account' is possible only for 'ecclesiastical faith', which, in its various forms, can be compared to 'pure religious faith' (p. 129). When the first accepts the need to 'conform' to the second, the *'church universal'* starts to become an 'ethical state of God' (p. 129). We have here a 'narrative' of 'conflict' between the 'faith of divine service' and that of 'moral religion', and this history will only 'have unity', if it focuses on the part of humanity that recognizes the difference between 'rational' and 'historical' faith (p. 130). So, we will limit ourselves to the Christian Church, which, from the outset, contained the 'objective unity of the true and *universal* religious faith to which it is gradually being brought nearer' (p. 130).

The '*Jewish faith*' has no 'essential connection' to it, despite coming 'immediately' before it (p. 130). 'Judaism' is not a 'religion', but a 'union' of members of a certain race, who submitted to 'purely political laws', to ensure that, if their 'secular state' were destroyed, there would be 'political faith' in the **Messiah**'s restoration of it (p. 130). Proof that this state was not a 'religious constitution' can be found in its laws, including those accompanying the '**Ten Commandments**', which were 'coercive' and 'external', making no claim on the '*moral disposition*' (p. 131). Although 'faith in a future life' arises 'automatically' in human beings, through their 'universal moral predisposition', it is absent from Judaism, indicating the intention to create a 'political', not an 'ethical' community (p. 131). Again, and at odds with the idea of establishing a '*church universal*', Judaism 'excluded the whole human race', so we should not attach much significance to the fact that it believed that one God was 'universal ruler of the universe': also, he was held to have demanded 'obedience to commands' in ways that required 'no improvement of moral disposition' (pp. 131–2).

Christianity was a 'revolution in doctrines of faith', and its teachers only linked it to Judaism as the best means of '*introducing*' a pure moral religion' (p. 132). For the '**teacher of the Gospel**' had declared 'servile faith' in 'professions and practices' to be 'inherently null', and that only 'moral faith', which proves its 'genuineness' in 'good life conduct', makes 'human beings holy'. After giving, to the lengths of an 'undeserved' death, an example that conformed to the 'prototype of a humanity well-pleasing to God', he was shown returning to 'heaven', although able to assure his disciples he would still be with them, 'even to the **end of the world**' (pp. 132–3).

In the Bible, 'miracles and mysteries' attest to this teaching, and they would be needed, if it concerned only the 'descent' and possible '**supramundane** rank of his person'; but, as it is part of a 'moral and soul-saving faith', these are not required (p. 133).

While the 'pure faith of reason' is 'its own proof', every 'historical' faith needs a '*learned public*', to document it, and thus ensure its continuation (pp. 133–4). Christianity's early history is 'obscure', and we do not know if its first followers were 'improved morally' (p. 134). But, from the time the Romans became interested in it, and gave it a learned public, there is little evidence of the 'beneficial effect' a 'moral religion' should have, but plenty of evidence of 'superstition', division and persecution (pp. 134–5). However, what shines through these terrible events, is that its 'true first purpose' was to introduce a 'pure religious faith' (p. 135). The problem was that, due to a 'bad propensity in human nature', what should have served, at the start, to 'introduce this pure faith' (to 'win over' to it, the 'nation' that was used to its 'old historical faith') became the 'foundation of a universal world-religion' (p. 135).

The best 'period' of 'church history' is '*The present*' (p. 135). We have only to let the 'seed of the true religious faith', now being 'sown in Christianity', 'grow unhindered', for the 'visible representation' of an 'invisible Kingdom of God on earth' to begin to develop (p. 135). In 'our part of the world', reason has freed itself from the 'burden of a faith' that is 'exposed to the arbitrariness of its interpreters', and started to accept '*moderation*' in relation to claims about 'revelation' (p. 135). There can be no doubt that the Bible contains much that is 'godly', and which may be 'divine revelation', while the 'union of human beings into one religion' cannot be achieved without it and an 'ecclesiastical faith based on it' (pp. 135–6).

As a 'new revelation', attested by 'miracles', is not to be expected, the appropriate course is to use the existing 'book' for 'ecclesiastical instruction', but not to compel people to have faith in it (p. 136). Further, as the 'sacred narrative' has been 'given to this faith', to provide a 'vivid presentation' of 'virtue striving toward holiness', it must always be used 'in the interest of morality'; it must be emphasized that 'true religion' is not about what God has done 'for our salvation', but what we must do to 'become worthy of it' (p. 136). And 'rulers' must not obstruct the 'diffusion of these principles', by endorsing particular '**ecclesiastical doctrines**'; this inhibits 'freedom', and may prevent an 'advance in goodness' (pp. 136–7).

The 'Kingdom of Heaven' can be depicted as a 'visible Kingdom of God on earth', governed by God's '**representative and vicar**', which brings 'happiness', as the 'rebels' against God, and 'their leader', are overcome (p. 137). What Jesus taught 'his disciples' about the kingdom of God, though, was from the 'moral side': about the 'merit of being citizens of a divine state' (p. 137). He told them what they must do, not just to achieve this for themselves, but to unite others in it, extending to the 'whole human race' (pp. 137–8). But he warned them to expect 'tribulations and sacrifices', not happiness, 'on earth'; their 'reward' would be in heaven (p. 138). However, the 'history of the church' concerning its 'final destiny' shows it as 'finally *triumphant*', and 'crowned with happiness here on earth' (p. 138). 'Separation' of the 'good from the evil' is portrayed as the 'final consequence of the establishment of the divine state' (p. 138). This 'state' is victorious over its enemies, who are gathered in hell, and all 'earthly life' ends, as death 'is destroyed', and '**immortality**' ('salvation' for one side, 'damnation' for the other) begins (p. 138). The 'form of a church is dissolved', and the 'vicar on earth' enters the 'same class' as humans, who are raised to him as 'citizens of Heaven', so '**God is all in all**' (p. 138). All this is a 'beautiful ideal of the **moral world-epoch**', which introducing 'true universal religion' will accomplish (p. 138). It can be *'foreseen'* as completed only 'in faith', but we can *'glimpse'* it in the 'continuous advance' toward the 'highest possible good on earth' (p. 138). While reason accords 'proper symbolic meaning' to the various elements, such as the 'announcement of the proximity of the end of the world', this does express the need for us 'always to be ready for it': to think of ourselves as 'actually the chosen citizens of a divine (ethical) state', for '**the Kingdom of God is within you**' (p. 139).

General Remark (pp. 140–7)

Enquiry into 'forms of faith', relating to 'religion', always encounters an underlying *'mystery'*, something *'holy'* that is a 'moral object' and an 'object of reason', which 'every individual' can recognize 'internally for practical use', but which cannot be 'communicated universally'; and faith in it should be regarded as a *'pure faith of reason'* (p. 140). That 'such mysteries' exist cannot be determined *'a priori* and objectively'; we have to search our 'moral predisposition', to see if any exist in us (p. 140). This will not give access to the *'grounds* of morality', but 'freedom', which the 'unconditional moral law' discloses to human beings, 'through the determination' of the 'power of choice', is 'no mystery', and it is its application to 'realization of the final moral end' that leads us 'to holy mysteries' (pp. 140–1). Alone, human beings cannot 'realize the idea of the **supreme good**', bound up with the 'moral disposition', either as it relates to happiness, or to the 'union' of human beings, required to achieve the end (p. 141). But, as they feel a 'duty' to further it, they feel compelled to belief in a 'moral ruler of the world', who can make the end 'possible' (p. 141).

Although we must think of God as having such attributes as omnipotence, so he can execute his will, our concern is not with 'his nature', but his relationship to us as 'moral beings' (p. 141). For our 'practical reason', we need faith in him as *'holy* lawgiver', *'**benevolent** ruler'* and *'just* judge' (p. 142). There is, in fact, no 'mystery' in this faith, which states 'God's moral bearing toward the human race' (p. 142). But, as this purification of the 'moral relation' between God and human beings was first 'made public' in Christian doctrine, it can be described as a 'revelation': of something that was a 'mystery' to human beings, through their 'own fault' (pp. 142–3). The revelation tells us, first, that as 'lawgiver', God is neither 'indulgent', nor *'despotic'*, but concerned with human beings' 'holiness'; second, that his 'goodness' is his attending first to their 'moral constitution', by which they can become *'well-pleasing'* to him, and only then to their inability to do so, unaided; and third, that his 'justice' is his limiting his 'generosity' to the condition that human beings keep the 'holy law', as far as they can 'measure up to it' (p. 143). In relation to this 'creed of faith', which embodies the 'whole of pure moral religion', it helps to think of the one God as, 'morally', three different 'personalities'. But, if the '**Trinity**' is regarded as what 'God is in himself', human beings cannot understand it, and it does not aid 'moral improvement' (p. 143). Three 'mysteries' are 'revealed to us' through our reason (p. 143).

(1) Our *'call'* to be 'citizens of an ethical state' (pp. 143–4). We can think of ourselves as subject to 'divine legislation' only as God's creatures (p. 144). But the 'principle of causality' tells us that creatures' only 'inner ground of action' is the one the

'producing cause' has put in them, so, as this 'external cause' determines our actions, they cannot be free (p. 144). Thus, we must think of ourselves as 'already existing free beings', not through our 'creation', but through a 'purely moral necessitation', which is only possible 'according to the laws of freedom', that is 'through a call' (p. 144). **(2)** The 'mystery of *satisfaction*' (p. 144). Human beings are 'corrupted', but if God's 'goodness' has called us to be members of the 'Kingdom of Heaven', he must be able to compensate for our 'inadequacy' from his 'own holiness' (p. 144). But reason demands that the 'required goodness' must come from us, and that no one can stand in for another, on the basis of the 'superabundance' of 'his merit' (p. 144). If we need to '*assume*' such a thing, it can only be for 'moral purposes' (p. 144). **(3)** The 'mystery of *election*' (p. 144). Even if there is this 'vicarious satisfaction', 'morally believing acceptance of it' indicates a 'determination of the will toward the good', which we cannot accomplish ourselves (p. 144). However, if 'heavenly *grace*' assists only some human beings, not on the basis of 'merit of works', but 'through some unconditional *decree*', electing some, but **reprobating** others, this does not suggest 'divine justice, and is an 'absolute mystery' (p. 144).

God has not revealed to us why 'moral good or evil' exists in the world; how good arises in human beings, if there is always 'evil' in them; or why some are 'excluded' from this: we would not '*understand*' it (p. 145). Although he has 'revealed his will' to us, 'through the moral law', God has not disclosed how 'free action occurs' (p. 145). But, as far as the 'objective rule of our conduct' is concerned, all we require is 'sufficiently revealed' and 'understandable' (p. 145). It would be 'presumptuous' to seek more information than knowing the moral law calls us to 'good life conduct'; that respect for the law encourages us to trust in 'this good spirit', and hope we can 'satisfy' him; and that we must always 'test' ourselves, as if we were going to face a judge (p. 145). The 'highest goal' of our 'moral perfection', which we can never reach, is 'love of the Law' (p. 146). In God, we can '*revere*' 'Father', '*Son*' and '*Holy Spirit*', and, though we cannot '*call*' upon him in this **multiform personality**' (it would suggest 'diversity', when God is 'single'; God's nature being 'threefold' is just part of an ecclesiastical faith's traditional doctrine), we can in the name of the 'object' he loves 'above all', and with which it is our duty to 'enter in moral union' (pp. 146–7).

Part IV: Concerning service and counterfeit service under the dominion of the good principle, or, Of religion and priestcraft (pp. 151–91)

In the '**world of the understanding**', a thing is 'already there', when the 'causes', capable of bringing it fully into being, are in place, even if its 'complete development', in the '**world of the senses**', lies in the future; and this applies to the 'dominion of the good principle' (p. 151). Setting up an 'ethical community', 'as a Kingdom of God', creates a 'stronger force' to resist 'attacks of the evil principle', but 'human beings' can only do so 'through *religion*', and, for this to 'be public', the kingdom must take the 'visible form of a *church*' (p. 151). God, as 'founder', is the 'author' of the Church's '*constitution*'; human beings, divided into administrators and the '*congregation*, subject to their laws', are its members and the 'authors' of its 'organization' (p. 152). Of course, the 'pure religion of reason' is an 'invisible church', and members of this 'ethical community' do not require '*officials*', as they 'receive their orders from the **highest lawgiver** individually' (p. 152). Every 'visible' church, based on 'statutory laws', can only be the 'true church', to the degree it embodies the 'principle of constantly coming closer to the pure faith of religion', which will ultimately lead to the 'ecclesiastical faith' being discarded (p. 152). Church 'officials', who do not take account of 'this end', and teach that ecclesiastical faith is 'alone **salvific**', give the Church ' "*counterfeit service*" ', running 'counter' to God's 'intention' (pp. 152–3).

First Part   Concerning the service of God in general (*pp. 153–64*)

Religion is recognizing our duties as 'divine commands'; '*revealed* **religion**' is needing to know something is a divine command before recognizing it as a duty; '*natural religion*' is vice versa (p. 153). A '*rationalist*' holds that only natural religion is 'morally necessary', a '*naturalist*', that there is no 'supernatural divine revelation'. A '*pure rationalist*' admits the existence of revelation, but not that it is necessary for religion, a 'pure **supernaturalist**' holds that it is (p. 154). When divided by its 'first origin', religion is either 'natural' or 'revealed', but, when divided by its capability for '*external communication*', is either '*natural religion*' (of which everyone can be 'convinced through his reason') or '*learned religion*' (of which others can be convinced by 'erudition') (p. 154). While its being natural is the 'essential characteristic' of a religion that should 'bind' human beings, communicability is an important indicator of its suitability to be a 'universal religion of humanity' (p. 154). A religion can be '*natural*, yet also *revealed*', if human beings could eventually have reached it by 'their reason', but not 'as early': revelation is then 'very advantageous' (p. 154). It does not diminish the religion's 'comprehensibility', and people can still use reason to convince themselves of 'its truth' (p. 154).

But some religions can only be thought of as 'revealed', and would 'disappear from the world', unless 'preserved' in 'holy books' (pp. 154–5). To make clear 'our ideas of a revealed religion in general', we shall consider a book that is 'interwoven' with 'ethical' teachings and 'related to reason', the New Testament, and 'expound the Christian religion' first as a 'natural', and then as a 'learned religion' (p. 155).

First Section of the First Part   The Christian religion as natural religion (pp. 155–60)

'Natural religion' (as morality, together with God, as the world's 'moral originator', and 'immortality') is a 'pure practical concept of reason', of which we can convince all human beings; we can also persuade them that its 'effect' is duty (pp. 155–6). This has the essential 'qualification' of the 'true church', 'validity for every human being', and so needs only 'teachers', not 'dignitaries' (p. 156). But, this 'rational religion of single individuals' cannot achieve 'universality', unless it takes the form of a 'visible' church, as a *community of believers'*, based on the 'principles of a pure religion' (p. 156). To be the '**founder of such a church**' assumes a '**fact and not just a concept of pure reason**' (p. 156). Let us assume that someone preached a 'universal religion of reason', and suggested 'forms and observances', as means of establishing a church on its 'principles'; we would accept that church as the 'true universal' one (pp. 156–7). He does not found the religion, as it is written in everyone's 'heart', but the 'first true *church*' (p. 157). He says that what pleases God is not 'observance' of 'ecclesiastical duties', but the 'pure moral disposition of the heart'; that God regards 'sins in thought' as being as bad as those in 'deed': for example, that '**hate**' is '**tantamount**

to killing'; and that 'holiness' should be human beings' 'goal' (p. 157). He teaches that these 'pure dispositions' should show themselves as '*deeds*', performed publicly 'for imitation', so that religion will gradually 'grow into a kingdom of God through its inner power' (p. 158). He expresses 'all duties' in the '*universal* rule' of doing them only from the 'incentive' of 'appreciation of duty itself' ('**love God**'), and in the '*particular* rule' of the human being's relation to others ('**Love every one as yourself**') (p. 158). He dismisses any hope that 'moral goodness' will descend as a 'heavenly gift', or that a 'higher moral influence' will compensate for the individual's lack of moral 'perfection' (p. 158). He promises the 'sacrifices', involved in 'moral conduct', will be rewarded, in a 'future world', but will differ, according as they were performed for reward or their 'own sake': acting '*prudently*' may comply with the 'moral law', but is not the same as acting '*morally*' (p. 159). This is a 'complete religion', which can be conveyed to human beings 'through their own reason' (pp. 159–60). Further, its 'possibility', as a 'prototype', has been demonstrated in 'an example', without the need for 'authentication' by miracles (p. 160). References to the '**Mosaic** law' are there only to make it more palatable to a people who, steeped in 'statutory **dogmas**', are unreceptive to the 'religion of reason' (p. 160).

Second Section   The Christian religion as a learned religion (pp. 160–4)

If there are 'necessary dogmas of faith' that have been revealed, and so cannot be cognized through reason, but which need to be preserved for future generations, they have to be 'documented' by the '*learned*' (p. 160). Christianity is both a '*rational*' and a '*revealed*' faith (p. 160). Reason tells us our 'life-conduct' can never justify us before God, but that we need to be so justified, and 'ecclesiastical observances' are no substitute for 'righteousness' (p. 161). But, where it is based on 'facts', not reason, Christianity is *'faith'*; and this is the 'foundation of a church', which must be served according to both its 'historical faith' and the 'practical and moral faith of reason' (p. 161). To the extent that it is a *learned* faith', based on 'history' and 'erudition', Christianity is not a *'free* faith' (p. 161). Were it a 'pure faith of reason', it would be, even though the 'moral laws upon which it is based as faith in a divine legislator command unconditionally' (p. 161).

As it has many 'unlearned' followers, Christianity needs 'scholars', as 'interpreters and preservers' of its 'doctrine of revelation' (pp. 161–2). But 'universal human reason' must be recognized as the 'supreme commanding principle' (p. 162). While this is 'true *service* of the church', under 'dominion of the good principle', putting 'revealed faith' before 'religion' is a *'counterfeit'* one, which reverses the 'moral order', and turns 'mere means' into things that are 'unconditionally commanded' (p. 162). Such a church is run, not by 'true *servants*', but 'high *officials*', who want to be accepted as the scripture's 'exclusive' interpreters, thus dislodging the 'pure religion of reason' from its position as 'highest interpreter', and who make use of 'scriptural scholarship' to serve the 'interests of ecclesiastical faith' (p. 162).

Christianity had the disadvantage of existing for over a 'generation' before it came to the attention of a 'learned public', so its early events lack their 'corroboration' (p. 163). But its 'advantage over Judaism' is that its *first teacher* is portrayed as preaching it as a 'moral', not a 'statutory', religion, and so it stands in 'closest proximity to reason', enabling it to be propagated without 'historical scholarship, at all times and

66

among all peoples' (p. 163). But, to help its dissemination, its early '*congregations*' interwove elements of Judaism with it, and these have become part of its 'essential articles of faith', to which 'tradition and interpretations' have been added (pp. 163–4). These cause difficulties: as is the case, if 'we seek religion not within us but from outside' (p. 164).

Second Part Concerning the counterfeit service of God in a statutory religion (pp. 164–82)

True religion consists only of 'laws'; we become aware of their 'unconditional necessity', through 'pure reason' (p. 164). 'Statutes', which our 'moral judgment' deems 'arbitrary', exist for 'the sake of a church'. It is a '*delusion of religion*' to think **'statutory faith'** is essential to God's service, as it is a 'counterfeit service' (p. 164).

1   Concerning the universal subjective ground of religious delusion (pp. 165–6)

'**Anthropomorphism**', which human beings cannot escape in their 'theoretical representation of God', has serious implications for 'morality' (p. 165). We fashion '*for ourselves*' a God, who demands less 'effort' from us in relation to 'our moral disposition' (p. 165). We claim that things we do, 'solely' to please God, such as '**penances, castigations, pilgrimages**', as long as they do not violate morality, show 'willingness to serve him'; the more useless, and less directed at 'universal moral improvement', such activities are, the 'holier they seem to be' (p. 165). God may not be 'served' by these deeds, but is believed to see 'good' in those who do them: they may be too 'weak to obey his moral commands', but make up for it by 'eagerness to obey' (pp. 165–6). Some of these activities may be 'closer to the moral form' than others, but this whole approach is a 'mere delusion of religion' (p. 166).

2   The moral principle of religion opposed to the delusion of religion (pp. 166–70)

This principle needs no 'proof': '*Apart from a good life-conduct, anything which the human being supposes that he can do to become well-pleasing to God is mere religious delusion and counterfeit service of God*' (p. 166). This does not reject the belief that there are things only God can do to make human beings 'well-pleasing to him' but, if the Church declares this 'mystery' to be 'revealed', it is a 'dangerous religious delusion' to hold that just professing it can make us 'well-pleasing to God' (pp. 166–7).

Reason tells us that, as long as we progress towards 'conformity to the law', in a 'disposition of true devotion to duty', we can hope God will supplement 'what lies outside' our power, although we will not know how (p. 167). And why would we want to know? Only to make of it a 'divine service', which might win heaven's favour, before exerting our 'own powers toward a good life-conduct' (pp. 167–8). There are '*no bounds*' to 'counterfeit service of God', whereby the individual 'offers everything' to God, except 'his moral disposition', in the hope it may be accepted instead (p. 168). No way of serving God 'mechanically', from church attendance to pilgrimage, is better than another, as each '**surrogate**' for 'moral service' is of 'equal worth'; but attaching the 'highest value' to the 'disposition to virtue' is no delusion, but an 'efficacious contribution to the world's highest good' (pp. 168–9).

The Church calls what human beings can accomplish,

through the 'strength of the principle of virtue', '*nature*', and what God does to 'supplement' our moral 'deficiency', '*grace*'; but it is '*enthusiasm*' to believe we can 'distinguish the effects' of the two (p. 169). We cannot recognize a 'supersensible object' in experience; the most we can say is that there must be effects of grace, to 'supplement the imperfection of our striving for virtue' (p. 169). '**Religious *superstition***' is the delusion that 'religious acts of cult' can justify us before God; '**religious *enthusiasm***' is the delusion of desiring to accomplish this by 'striving for a supposed contact with God' (pp. 169–70). '**Superstitious delusion**' ('superstitious', because the means selected are 'natural', not 'moral', and cannot affect the 'ethical good', which is not natural) is the desire to be well-pleasing to God, without becoming a 'good human being', as, for example, in 'ecclesiastical' observances; '**enthusiastic' delusion** is when the means selected are 'supersensible' and outside human power (p. 170). While 'superstitious delusion' just turns what can be no more than a means into an 'object immediately well-pleasing to God', 'enthusiastic religious delusion' causes the 'moral death of the reason', without which there can be no religion (p. 170). To avert 'religious delusion', 'ecclesiastical faith' must have the principle of 'bringing about the religion of good life conduct as its true goal' (p. 170).

3 Concerning priestcraft as a regime in the counterfeit service of the good principle (pp. 170–8)

When 'servile worship' of 'God (or **idols**)' took 'public and legal form', it became '*temple service*', and then '*ecclesiastical service*' (pp. 170–1). But serving God through 'faith in certain statutory articles' cannot make 'a better human being' (p. 171). Only those whose service is the 'disposition to good life conduct', embrace the principle that declares them members of the '(invisible) church' (p. 171). 'Moral service' alone is directly pleasing to God: actions with 'no moral value in themselves' can be seen as well-pleasing to God, only insofar as they further the *'moral service of God'* (p. 172).

Human beings performing actions devoid, in themselves, of anything well-pleasing to God, to gain his favour, are under the 'delusion' they can secure a 'supernatural effect', through 'natural means' (p. 172). This is *'sorcery'*, or *'fetishism'* (p. 172). It is one thing if, as well as an 'active disposition to a good life-conduct', the individual follows certain 'observances', merely to make himself *'worthy'* of 'supernatural assistance' for 'attainment of the object of his morally good wish'; he is not then trying to do something to 'influence' the 'divine will', but to receive something he cannot 'produce himself' (pp. 172–3). But, when 'precedence' is given to observing 'statutory laws', based on 'revelation', which are said to be 'necessary to religion', not as a 'means to the moral disposition', but as a way of becoming 'well-pleasing to God directly', and when 'the historical faith' is put ahead of 'good life-conduct', the 'service of God' becomes 'mere *fetishism*' (p. 173). *'Priestcraft'* is the nature of a church, ruled by *'fetish-service'*, whose 'essence' is 'statutory commands', rather than 'principles of morality'; and it will always be 'despotic', robbing 'the masses' of their 'moral freedom' (p. 174). Where there are 'articles of faith', there will be *'clergy'* who, as interpreters of God's will, 'dispense with reason' and, in the end, 'scriptural scholarship itself'; and as, apart from the ruler of the state, there is only the *'laity'*, the church, through its influence over their minds, 'rules the state' as well (p. 174).

Now, it is not just the 'learned', who need to be 'capable of this faith', and it might seem that 'historical faith', with its 'accessible' narrative, is particularly well suited to those 'limited conceptually' (p. 175). However, there is a 'practical cognition', which, though it depends on reason alone, is as 'close to every human being, even the simplest', as if it had been 'inscribed in his heart': the 'law of morality' (p. 175). And this leads to 'faith in God', or certainly to the idea of him as 'moral legislator', and thus to 'pure religious faith' (p. 175). Our duty is to make this the 'supreme condition' of taking part in 'whatever salvation' a 'historical faith' offers: although this does not stop the 'moral believer' being 'open to historical faith', insofar as it contributes to the 'vitality of his pure religious disposition' (pp. 175–6).

Even when a church serves God by aiming at 'pure moral veneration', according to 'the laws prescribed to humanity in general', the question arises of whether the principal element in 'religious instruction' should be the '***doctrine of divine blessedness***', or the 'pure ***doctrine of virtue***' (p. 176). The first consists of two 'determinations of the moral disposition' towards God: '*fear*', 'obedience to his commands from *imposed* duty'; and '*love*', obeying from 'one's own *free choice*' (p. 176). Both involve, as well as 'morality', the 'concept of a supersensible being', who 'transcends our faculties', and who, when we go beyond his 'moral relation' to us, can be understood 'anthropomorphically', and so in a way that is 'prejudicial to our ethical principles' (p. 176). There is the risk that church education and preaching will give the 'doctrine of divine blessedness' priority over that of 'virtue': but it is the second that is the 'end', and which 'stands on its own (even without the concept of God)'; the first is only a 'means' (p. 176). 'Divine blessedness' cannot constitute of itself 'the final end of moral striving'; it is only a way of reinforcing what makes for a 'better human being': 'virtuous disposition' (pp. 176–7). It does so by offering to this 'striving' the 'expectation of the final end for which it is itself powerless' (p. 177).

The 'concept of virtue' fosters a sense of human 'dignity', and leads to God, who is 'worthy of adoration', only as the 'legislator of virtue' (p. 177). The danger of starting with a 'world ruler', who makes 'duty a commandment', is that this can turn 'divine blessedness' into 'slavish subjection to the commands of a despotic might' (p. 177). The **doctrine of atonement** follows from our 'courage' to stand on our own feet, and strengthens it, by showing 'what cannot be altered as wiped out', and laying open the path to 'new conduct of life' (p. 177). But, if it comes first, the focus on hopelessly trying to undo 'what has been done (expiation)', the sense of 'incapacity for the good' and fear of falling back 'into evil', strip away our courage (p. 177). If we subordinate virtue to 'reverence for God', he becomes an '*idol*', whom we 'hope to please', not by 'morally upright conduct', but 'adoration' (p. 178). Divine blessedness is not a 'surrogate for virtue', but its 'completion', providing the 'hope of the final success of all our good ends' (p. 178).

4 Concerning the guiding thread of conscience in matters of faith (pp. 178–82)

How can '**conscience**' guide us in 'perplexing moral decisions' (p. 178)? It is '*a consciousness which is of itself a duty*'. Generally, 'understanding', not conscience, decides whether an action is 'right or wrong' (p. 179). But, with an action '*I* want to undertake', I must be '*certain*' it is right, and this is a 'requirement of conscience' that opposes '***probabilism***' (p. 179). It does not usurp the role of reason, and judge actions in relation to the moral law; it is reason judging itself, as to whether it has adequately scrutinized the rightness or wrongness of actions.

An '**inquisitor**' is sure that a 'supernaturally revealed divine will' orders him to 'extirpate' religious dissent, and he condemns a 'heretic' to death (p. 179). But his certainty of this being God's will is based on 'historical documentation'; it is not '**apodictically certain**' (p. 179). It would be wrong, and acting 'unconscientiously', to 'destroy a human being' on this basis (pp. 179–80). The clergy act against their consciences, if they use their 'spiritual authority' to force others to believe in such things as religious mysteries, which are beyond their understanding, and of which they cannot be 'wholly convinced' themselves; and must accept responsibility when such a 'servile faith' leads to abuses (p. 180). While those, like '**Protestants**', who are free of a 'slavish yoke of faith', feel they can believe 'less', the opposite is the case with those who are not (p. 181). They think it desirable to adopt the 'security maxim in matters of faith', and 'believe too much rather than too little' (p. 181). The right approach is to treat religious beliefs that derive from revelation, but which are not at odds with 'pure principles of morality', as not certainly true or false, but as likely to be 'saving', only if a person has not made himself 'unworthy', through a 'defect' in his 'moral disposition' (p. 181). This is 'true moral safety': 'safety before conscience' (p. 181). It is not in keeping with 'conscientiousness' to impose allegedly 'divinely revealed' propositions on people as duties, when doing so will probably crush the freedom necessary for 'everything moral' (p. 182).

Detailed Summary

General Remark (pp. 182–91)

The 'good' human beings can do, 'according to the laws of freedom', without 'supernatural help', can be described as *'nature'*, as distinct from *'grace'* (p. 182). The former term does not imply a 'physical property distinct from freedom', and is used simply because we are cognisant, through reason, of the *'laws* of this faculty': those of *'virtue'* (p. 182). But, as with everything 'supernatural' to which, as *'holiness'*, morality belongs, the extent of grace's effect on us is 'hidden' (p. 183). 'Supernatural intervention' in our moral 'faculty', to 'satisfy our duty', is a **transcendent concept**, outside 'experience' (p. 183). It is problematic, because reason tells us we gain credit only for 'good conduct', attributable to our 'own powers': but, the 'possibility' of freedom is itself equally 'incomprehensible' (p. 183). As we cannot know anything about the operation of grace, or when to expect its assistance, we should not think about it, in case we disable ourselves from the 'use of reason', or become inactive, through expecting from God what we should be 'seeking within us' (p. 183). The idea of a *'means of grace'* is 'self-contradictory': we cannot become 'worthy of heavenly assistance', except by improving our 'moral nature', to fit ourselves for 'divine approval' (pp. 183–4). True service of God is *'service of the heart'*, and is as 'invisible' as his 'kingdom'; it lies in the 'disposition of obedience to all true duties as divine commands', not in actions carried out 'exclusively for God' (p. 184). However, human beings need to give this 'invisible' service a 'visible' form: which then comes to be regarded as the actual service (p. 184).

Four 'observances' foster 'attention to the true service of God' (p. 184). 'Private prayer' helps fix *'this good firmly within us'*; 'church-going' promotes it, by broadcasting 'religious doctrines'; *'baptism'* transmits it to 'posterity', through receiving new members of the 'fellowship'; and **'communion'** maintains this, and cements the Church's members into an 'ethical body' (pp. 184–5). A practice, not performed in a 'purely moral spirit', but to propitiate God, is *'fetish-faith'* (p. 185). But, even when humans see that everything depends on 'moral good', originating in action, they still look for a way around this 'arduous condition', hoping that God will treat observing *'the custom'* as doing the 'act itself': hence, the development of 'certain practices' as *'means of grace'* (p. 185). There are 'three kinds of *delusory faith*': 'faith *in miracles*', believing we cognize things that cannot happen 'according to objective laws of experience'; 'faith *in mysteries*', things of which we can 'form no concept through reason'; and 'faith in *means of grace*': that, by 'purely natural means', we can bring God's 'influence' to bear on 'our morality' (p. 185). The first two are dealt with above. The third must be distinguished from the *'effects of grace*, i.e. supernatural moral influences', to which we are 'passively related' (pp. 185–6).

(1) *'Praying'* is a 'superstitious delusion', if regarded as an *'inner ritual* service of God', and thus a 'means of grace' (p. 186). God already knows our wishes, and it discharges none of our duties. The *'spirit of prayer'*, the desire to 'please God' in all we do, should always be 'in us', but expressing it in 'words and formulas' cannot satisfy God (pp. 186–7). Religious people are too inclined to turn everything 'connected with their personal moral improvement' into **'courtly service'** (p. 188). It is important to teach children, who need the 'letter' of prayer, that 'speech' is not valuable 'in itself', but only to stimulate the 'disposition to a life-conduct well-pleasing to God' (p. 188). (2) *'Church-going'* is not only 'valuable' as a means of individual *'edification'*, but also strengthens people's consciousness of being 'citizens of a divine state which is to be

represented here on earth' (pp. 188–9). But thinking of it as a means of grace, as if it served God 'directly', is a 'delusion' that diminishes, rather than enhances, the 'quality of the citizen as *citizen in the Kingdom of God*' (p. 189). **(3)** Receiving a '*member into a church*' is a solemn occasion, which 'imposes grave obligations' on the 'initiate', or (if a child) those responsible for him; but it is not a 'holy action' that makes the baptized person receptive to 'divine grace' (p. 189). **(4)** '*Communion*' follows the 'example' of the Church's 'founder', emphasizes the idea of a 'cosmopolitan *moral community*', and encourages the church community to the 'moral disposition of brotherly love' (pp. 189–90). But, seeing it as a means of grace is a delusion that can only 'work counter to the spirit of religion' (p. 190). In general, '*Priestcraft*' is the 'dominion' the clergy have gained over church members' minds, by claiming 'exclusive possession of the means of grace' (p. 190).

In relation to God's 'moral properties' of 'holiness, mercy, and justice', human beings appeal to the second, to avoid complying with the demands of the first (p. 190). It is hard work to be a 'good *servant*', who has to discharge duties, less arduous to be a '*favorite*' who is 'forgiven' much (p. 190). They appeal 'exclusively' to God's '*grace*', and apply themselves to every possible religious 'formality', showing respect for his commands, in the hope they will not have to '*observe*' them (p. 190). They leave the job of making themselves better human beings to God, while focusing on '**piety**' (mere 'passive respect of the divine law'), not '*virtue*' (actually carrying out duties) (p. 191). The two must be combined to produce a truly '*religious disposition*' (p. 191). But, if people become convinced they possess 'special effects of faith', virtue can become 'loathsome' to them (p. 191). It is no surprise people are often said not to be improved by religion, and that their supposed 'inner light' seldom manifests itself in 'good works' (p. 191). The 'teacher of the Gospel' has told us that we can 'recognize' people 'by their fruits' (p. 191). At present, there is no evidence that the so-called religious 'elect' will outperform those 'naturally honest human beings' who can be depended upon in 'daily affairs', 'business' and 'need' (p. 191).

Overview

The following section is a chapter-by-chapter overview of the four chapters in Kant's *Religion within the Boundaries of Mere Reason*, designed for quick reference to the detailed summary above. Readers may also find this section helpful for revision.

Prefaces (pp. 33–41)

As morality is based on the idea that human beings are free, but also bind themselves, through their reason, by moral laws, no superior being is needed to make them recognize their duty, or offer them rewards, to get them to do it. Morality is independent of religion, but does need to address the question of consequences. Human beings have an idea of a highest good, in which happiness is proportioned to the performance of duty, and which only an all-powerful God can make possible. Morality leads to religion but, as human beings diminish even sublime things, it is expressed in forms which depend for their authority on coercive laws, and is subject to censorship. Religious censors should not stifle scholarship and research, but should give philosophical theology free rein (as long as it does not invade the province of biblical theology), and listen to what philosophers have to say.

Part I (pp. 45–73)

There are two opposed views of the world: that it is dominated by physical and moral evil; or that it is going from bad to better, and that, just as human beings' bodies are sound by nature, so are their souls. But experience does not support the latter theory. Human beings could be partly good and partly evil, but it is hard to tell because, although actions that are contrary to the moral law can be identified, it is not possible to observe the maxims on which they are based. The word 'nature' suggests the opposite of free actions, but refers only to the subjective ground of the exercise of the human being's freedom, which must be a deed of freedom, if he is to be held responsible for his choices. The good or evil in him would not be moral, if his exercise of freedom could be attributed to natural causes. Saying a particular human being is good or evil, by nature, just means that he has within him a first ground for adopting good or evil maxims; and, although this is innate in a human being, he is its author.

Remark (pp. 47–50) It could be a false antithesis to say that human beings are, by nature, either morally good or evil: they may be both good and evil. But the distinctive characteristic of freedom of the power of choice is that nothing can determine it to action, unless the human being has made it a universal rule, by which he wills to conduct himself. To be good in one part is to have incorporated the moral law into one's maxim, so one who adopts the moral law as his maxim is morally good, while one who incorporates deviation from it into his maxim is evil. That these two dispositions are innate does not mean a human being is not the author of his particular disposition, but that he has not acquired it in time, and so has always had it.

I (pp. 50–2) The human being is predisposed to good as a living, rational and responsible being, and, as a rational and responsible being, he is open to respect for the moral law within him. However, he is liable to such vices as lust and lawlessness, while his desire for others' good opinion can result in an unjust desire to gain superiority over them, giving rise to envy and ingratitude.

II (pp. 52–5) Human beings' natural tendency to moral evil belongs to them universally, and they can be thought of as having brought it on themselves. There are three grades of it: human frailty (general weakness in complying with the maxims of the moral law); impurity (needing incentives, other than those of the moral law, to perform duties); and depravity (subordinating the incentives of the moral law to non-moral ones). As it is woven into human nature, it exists in even the best human beings. A human being's actions may comply with the moral law but, if his moral choice is determined by such incentives as ambition or even sympathy, their doing so is accidental. The maxim, by the goodness of which his moral worth must be measured, is contrary to the moral law, and so, despite good actions, he is evil. The propensity to evil is not physical, as it originates from freedom, and relates to the human being's power of choice as a moral being. But only a deed for which human beings are responsible can be morally evil and, as a propensity is a determining ground of the power of choice, which precedes every deed, it is not yet one. However, there are two senses of deed: the use of freedom, by which the supreme maxim, whether for or against the moral law, is adopted in the power of choice, and the actions that result from adopting it. The tendency to evil is the first kind of deed, and is the basis of every deed that is contrary to moral law. While the second is an empirical deed, occurring in time, the first is an intelligible one, known through reason. It is innate, as it cannot be eradicated: for that, the supreme maxim would need to be good. Although it is human beings' own deed, they do not know why evil has corrupted their very highest maxim.

III (pp. 55–61) Saying human beings are evil means they are conscious of the moral law, but have incorporated deviations from it into their maxims. To be morally evil, and something human beings can be held accountable for, this propensity cannot be a natural predisposition, but must come about through their own fault. It is a radical innate evil in human nature, the ground of which cannot lie in a human being's natural inclinations, as it relates to him as a free being. However, it cannot be located in corruption of the morally legislative reason itself, as it would be contradictory to think of human beings as freely acting beings, but not subject to the moral law. The worst human being does not repudiate the moral law: his moral predisposition means it imposes itself on him irresistibly and, were there no other factors, he would make it his supreme maxim, and be morally good. But he incorporates incentives of his physical nature into his maxim, and, if he allowed these wholly to determine his choice, without heeding the moral law, would be morally evil. What happens is that human beings incorporate both into the same maxim, so their being good or evil depends on which predominates. But even when human beings' maxims are contrary to the moral law, their actions can still comply with it, as when someone finds it easier to be honest than to tell lies. This propensity is morally evil; radical, as it corrupts the grounds of all maxims; and cannot be eliminated by human means, as it assumes the subjective ground of all maxims to be corrupted. However, it must be possible to overcome it, as it is found in the human being acting freely. It is a perversity, which is called evil, due to its results, and it derives from human frailty. Human beings' innate guilt, which can be spotted in their first exercise of freedom, but which originates from it, and for which they are accountable, can, at one level, be considered unintentional, but is deliberate, at a deeper level, when human beings deceive themselves as to whether their disposition is evil, provided its actions do not produce evil. This dishonesty impedes development of a genuine moral disposition.

IV (pp. 61–5) If, as with moral evil, an effect is related to a cause by laws of freedom, it is not related to it in time: free actions do not have a temporal origin. But, whatever the origin of moral evil in human beings, the least satisfactory way of explaining it is to think of it as inherited from our ancestors. An action must always be regarded as an original exercise of the power of choice, and, whatever natural causes the human agent is subject to, an evil action is free, and he is accountable for it. It is not possible to investigate such a deed's origin in time, only its origin in reason, and then attempt to explain why there is this propensity to evil. Genesis depicts evil's origin, not in a fundamental propensity to it, which would prevent it being the result of freedom, but in sin: contravening the moral law as a divine command. The human being started to question it, subordinating the incentive of the law to other aims, and including these in his maxim. Evil can have originated only from moral evil but, as human beings' original predisposition, which only they could have corrupted, if they are to be held responsible for it, is to the good, it is impossible to explain how moral evil first came into us. The Bible locates evil's origin in Satan, but this does not make it more understandable. But, by showing human beings as giving in to temptation, it shows them, in contrast to Satan, as not fundamentally corrupted and, as they possess a good will, capable of returning to good.

General Remark (pp. 65–73) To say human beings are created good means that this is their original predisposition, and that they determine whether they will be good or evil, by whether or not they incorporate the incentives of that predisposition into their maxims. If this requires supernatural assistance, they must make themselves worthy of, and accept, it. Despite their fall, they are aware of the command that they ought to become better, so there is a germ of goodness in them. Regaining the original disposition to good means making the moral law the supreme ground of all their maxims, and not subordinating them to inclinations. Habitually complying with duty is virtue in its empirical character, which does not require a change of heart; virtue, in its intelligible character, is not to need any incentive to recognize a duty, except duty itself, which can only be achieved by a revolution in the disposition. It is hard to see how, if he is corrupt in the very ground of his maxims, a human being can, by himself, become a good human being. He must change the supreme ground of his maxims, and will only become good by unremitting effort. For God, who knows the intelligible ground of the heart, this is the same as his actually being a good human being. Gradually, duty for its own sake will become an attitude of mind and, while it seems incomprehensible that human beings can restore their good predisposition, through their own efforts, despite being innately corrupt, if the moral law commands that they ought to be better, they must be capable of it. They cannot obtain evidence of this transformation, as they cannot penetrate the depths of their heart, but they can hope their efforts will take them in the right direction. They ought to become good human beings, and can only be judged morally good on the basis of what they achieve themselves. Cultic religions can mislead, by teaching that God will remit human beings' debts, and make them eternally happy, without their needing to become better. But, Christianity, a moral religion, teaches that God's help is only available if they make an effort. As to the effects of grace, it is an issue that, like all supernatural questions, falls outside the limits of reason. Further, expecting an effect of grace would mean that our becoming morally good was not our own doing, but that of another being.

Part II (pp. 77–102)

To become a morally good human being, the cause of evil must be combated. This does not lie in the natural inclinations, which are good in themselves, and just need to be controlled, but in the power of choice and not recognizing that failing to struggle with the inclinations is contrary to duty.

Section 1 (pp. 79–93)

A (pp. 79–81) The only thing that can make the world the end of God's creation is humanity in its full moral perfection. The idea of such a human being proceeds from God's being: he is God's only-begotten Son. Human beings can become God's children, by adopting his dispositions, and it is their duty to raise themselves to this ideal. However, it is more comprehensible to say that this prototype came down from heaven, and, for the world's good, endured its sufferings. But human beings are never free of guilt, even after adopting the same disposition. Moral perfection can only be conceived as the idea of a human being prepared, despite temptations, to carry out all human duties; to spread goodness, by teaching and example; and to suffer for the world's sake. Only through faith in the Son of God can human beings hope to be pleasing to God.

B (pp. 81–4) The moral law commands unconditionally and, even though no one had ever been able so to obey it, the need for one who can is self-evident. Such an example need not be drawn from experience; it is present in the reason. Indeed, only faith in the idea in the reason has moral worth. If a human being had come down from heaven, at a particular point in history, and accomplished great moral good, through a revolution in human beings, there would be no reason to think he was not a normally born human, who was leading an exemplary life. His divine origin would have no practical advantage, as ordinary human beings must seek the prototype they see in him in themselves. Placing him above the frailty of human nature makes him harder to emulate, as the gap between him and ordinary humans seems so great. People might say that a holy will, and certainty of eternal glory, would enable them to resist temptations, and endure suffering and death. Although human beings should follow his example, he could not be put forward as proof that they could reach this level of moral goodness. But when a teacher is an irreproachable example of what he teaches, and it is everyone's duty to do likewise, it must be ascribed to his having the purest disposition, and one that is valid for all humans, at all times, and in all places.

C (pp. 84–93) The Bible teaches human beings to be holy, like God. But there is a gulf between the goodness they should bring about in themselves, and the evil from which they begin. Yet, their moral makeup should be in accord with this holiness, which must be present in their disposition, as the germ from which all good can be developed, and which flows from their adopting a holy principle as their supreme maxim. Such a change of heart must be possible, as it is a duty, but it is hard to see how the disposition can count for the deed itself, when the latter is always defective. But, while human beings only see themselves as gradually progressing towards something better, God treats their infinite progress towards conformity with the moral law as a perfected whole: so they can be well-pleasing to God, whenever their lives end. There is also the issue of whether they can be certain that their disposition will enable them always to advance in goodness. But such certainty would be like knowing they were already in possession of God's kingdom, and could be sure of a full measure of physical happiness: morality gains from people having to work out their salvation in fear and trembling. Without confidence in their disposition, though, they will be discouraged from persisting. They must observe their steady improvement, since adopting good principles, and from this infer improvement in their disposition, which will give them assurance of being able to persevere in this life and the next. If someone goes from bad to worse, he will have to conclude that corruption is rooted in his disposition. The first is the glimpse of an endlessly happy future, the second, of an equally miserable one. This will reassure some, while spurring others on to break with evil. Complete certainty is neither possible, nor morally beneficial. Starting from evil creates a debt. Moral evil, called sin when the moral law is taken as a divine command, involves an infinite number of breaches of it, and so an infinite amount of guilt. Thus, every human being should expect infinite punishment. But, while he deserved punishment before conversion, his good disposition now predominates, so it is not appropriate. However, as supreme justice cannot allow one who deserves punishment, not to be, it must be regarded as adequately executed in the conversion. This is both an exit from sin and an entry into goodness but, as evil can only be set aside through adopting the good disposition, it is one, not two, moral acts.

Exchanging the corrupted disposition for the good involves sacrifice and punishment, as the new human being has to endure all life's ills. Physically, it is the same human being, who deserves punishment, but, as an intelligible being, he is now, in God's eyes, another being morally. This new disposition, personified as the Son of God, bears his debt of sin for him. The suffering the new human being must undergo is shown as a death suffered once and for all by human beings' representative, and is imputed to human beings by grace, as if already possessed. But the important point is that the individual has the required good disposition, and understands that his only hope of being absolved from the burden of guilt is through a total change of heart. As to what he can expect when life ends, he must take his whole life into account, not just the last, and best, part. The judge within him will be stern, but human beings are too ready to use the excuse of human frailty. If they believe that all will be well, they will just hope to get their lives in order by the time they end.

Section 2 (pp. 94–8)

In the Bible, two opposed principles test their powers on the human being. God makes him proprietor of the earth's goods, but an evil being successfully tempts Adam and Eve, thus establishing himself as prince of this world. God does not wipe out this evil kingdom, as he abides by the principle of freedom in his dealings with rational beings. The Jewish theocracy gave the good principle a foothold in the world, but its laws were only partly ethical, and it did not address the issue of the moral disposition. Then came one who presented himself as a true human being, but also of heavenly origin, and not part of human beings' bargain with the evil principle. Feeling threatened, the prince of this world caused him to suffer persecution and a shameful death. But the principles of good and evil have power in the realm of freedom, not nature, and Jesus' death gave an example of humanity in its moral perfection for others to follow.

In fact, this good principle has been present from the beginning of the human race, but, by exemplifying it, Jesus opened the doors of freedom to all who choose to renounce everything that keeps them tied to earthly life, to the detriment of morality. The evil principle is not beaten but, as human beings have been shown another moral realm, where they can find freedom, its power to control them, against their will, is ended.

However, as the evil principle remains prince of this world, adherents of the good principle must expect persecution. The message of this story is that human beings' salvation depends on their adopting genuine moral principles in their disposition; that it is perversity that stops them; but, if they embrace the idea of the moral good fully, the powers of evil cannot prevail against it. However, they must not follow superstitious practices: the good's only distinguishing quality is well-ordered life-conduct.

General Remark (pp. 98–102)

A moral religion that treats human duties as divine commands does not need miracles, but, when a religion of the moral disposition replaces one of cult and observances, they may help it to be accepted. Even when the true religion can hold its own on rational grounds, there is no need to challenge them, although belief in them will not make people well-pleasing to God. God is the world's ruler and creator, according to both the order of nature and the moral order. If he allows nature to deviate from such laws, we cannot know why he does so, but should just accept that he always does what is good. Practically, miracles cannot affect how we use our reason. For example, whatever a judge may profess in church, he ignores the offender's claim of being tempted by the devil. Although human moral improvement may be affected by heavenly influences, there is no criterion by which to identify them, or distinguish them from natural ones. We must follow reason, and behave as if all moral improvement results from our own efforts.

Part III (pp. 105–47)

The most that the morally well-disposed human being can achieve in his battle with the evil principle is to be free of its control, and live for righteousness. One problem is that human beings corrupt each other's moral disposition, making each other evil. The good principle's victory over the evil one can only be achieved by creating a society in conformity with laws of virtue. This ethical community or state can exist within the political one.

Division 1 (pp. 106–29)

I (pp. 106–8) In a political state, human beings are subject to coercive laws, in an ethico-civil one only to laws of virtue.

Members of the first may wish to have the dispositions to virtue that coercion cannot provide. Indeed, coercion would prevent creation of an ethical community, by subverting its ends: the citizens of the political community must be totally free to enter, or not enter, an ethical union.

II (pp. 108–9) Just as human beings should refrain from injustice and war, and enter a politico-civil state, they should adopt the same approach to the ethical state of nature, in which the principles of virtue battle with inner immorality. They have a duty, as rational beings, to promote the highest good as a good common to all. Individuals cannot do this alone. A union of well-disposed human beings is needed, to build a universal state, based on laws of virtue. This may not be in their power: a higher moral being may be required, to unite the forces of single individuals.

III (pp. 109–10) A community under coercive laws is not an ethical one: the latter's laws concern what is internal, the morality of actions. Ethical laws cannot derive originally from the will of a superior lawgiver, as this would make the duty to obey them, not a matter of free virtue, but a legal duty. In an ethical community, the supreme lawgiver must be one, in relation to whom ethical duties can be represented as his commands, and who knows each person's disposition. This is God, the world's moral ruler, and an ethical community is only conceivable as a people of God, acting in conformity with laws of virtue.

IV (pp. 111–12) Only God, not human beings, can fully realize the idea of an ethical community. But they must behave as if everything depended on them. An ethical community that is not an object of possible experience (one in which all upright human beings join under direct, yet moral, divine rule, and which is a model for one humans found) is called the Church invisible. The Church visible is the actual union of human beings, in accord with this idea. The true visible Church shows God's moral kingdom on earth, as far as human beings can achieve it. It is universal, and so there are no internal divisions; pure, as it has only moral incentives and no superstition; its internal relations and those with the state are free; and it operates according to definite principles with clear rules of instruction. An ethical community's constitution is not like a political one, but more like that of a family, with an invisible moral father, whose son, related by blood to the family members, tells them of the father's will; and they honour the father in him, and enter a free, universal and lasting union of hearts.

V (pp. 112–17) A universal Church can only be based on rational religious faith, but human beings find it hard to accept that the service God wants from them is steadfast pursuit of a morally good life, in which they do their duty to others. They feel they must perform some service to God, even though it lacks moral value. The result is a religion of divine service, rather than a purely moral one. God is the lawgiver, to be honoured universally, and he commands through either statutory or moral laws. With the latter, we can recognize God's will, through reason: indeed, the idea of God comes from consciousness of these laws. But statutory laws can be known only through revelation, which gives a historical, not a rational, faith. And, even if there are divine statutory laws, the moral law is the condition of all true religion; the former can only be the means of promoting it.

However, reason seems unable to tell people how to honour

God in church: this requires definite rules, derived from revelation, giving rise to ecclesiastical, as opposed to pure religious, faith. When it is set up, it is rash to think a church's rules are immediately divine and statutory, though arrogant to deny that a special authority underlies its organization, especially if it harmonizes with moral religion. The fact is that human beings gravitate towards a religion of divine service, based on revelation, and direct worship of God, rather than one of conformity to his moral commands, prescribed through reason. They do not regard the means of promoting the moral content of religion, such as religious ceremonies, as necessary in themselves, but as ways of serving God. Although lacking moral value, they are thought to please him, because done for his sake. If a statutory ecclesiastical faith is not added to pure religious faith, to promote it, the latter's preservation cannot be achieved through tradition, but only through scripture; and it is fortunate when the holy book also contains the pure moral doctrine of religion. There is only one true religion, and this can be found in different churches, so it is better to talk of different faiths than different religions.

VI (pp. 118–22) By being based on revelation, a church loses its claim to universality, but human beings need something their senses can grasp, to support even the highest concepts. Therefore, ecclesiastical faith is necessary; but it must be interpreted in a way that harmonizes with the universal rules of a pure religion of reason, so that it teaches people to treat human duties as divine commands. Greek and Roman moral philosophers reinterpreted stories about their gods as symbolic portrayals of God's attributes, and such reinterpretation is acceptable, provided it is not claimed that it conveys the stories' precise original meaning. Exposition of, and scholarly research into, scripture should relate its contents to pure moral faith, and enable uneducated church members to understand it, and draw appropriate lessons from it. This work must be free of state interference. Scripture must not be interpreted on the basis of inner feelings, which are not a reliable means of recognizing that laws are moral, or identifying direct divine influence. They promote undesirable religious enthusiasm, and can undermine the standing of moral feeling. Scripture is the only norm of ecclesiastical faith, and the religion of reason and scholarship its only expositor; but only the first is valid for the whole world. In the end, ecclesiastical faith is just faith in scholars, making it all the more important that these allow public scrutiny and debate of their interpretations.

VII (pp. 122–9) Universality is the distinguishing mark of a true church; but, if a historical faith can get ever closer to the pure religion of faith, based on reason, until it can be set aside as its vehicle, it may be regarded as the true one, even though it is not a moral one, and hopes to please God by actions that lack moral worth. A saving faith has two conditions for its hope of blessedness: the lawful undoing, before a judge, of actions done, which it cannot accomplish itself; and conversion to a new life that complies with duty, which it can. The former is faith in redemption, the latter, in becoming well-pleasing to God, through good conduct. They are connected necessarily, but this can only be seen if it is assumed, either that faith in our being absolved from the debt of sin will lead to good life conduct, or that the active disposition of the second will lead to faith in our absolution. This contradiction needs to be resolved, to decide whether historical faith is actually a crucial part of saving faith over and above the pure religious one, or whether it will ultimately pass over into the latter.

1 If satisfaction has been made for human sins, and, if availing oneself of it were just a matter of faith, every sinner would do so. But it is hard to see how any rational human being, knowing he deserves punishment, could accept that his guilt has been removed, and good life-conduct will follow, just by believing that satisfaction has been made. It is only possible, if the faith is thought of as coming from heaven, and that reason does not need to explain it further. One who cannot do so must think of it as conditional, and regard improvement in his life conduct as having to come first. But, if historical knowledge of the favour is part of ecclesiastical faith, but improved life conduct part of pure moral faith, the latter must take precedence.

2 If the human being is corrupt by nature, and still in the power of the evil principle, it seems impossible that he should believe himself capable of becoming a new man. If he cannot see himself as reconciled through the satisfaction made for him, and thus able to lead a new life, faith in merit that is not his own must come before striving for good works, contradicting the previous proposition. This is an insoluble problem, but human beings must start from what they ought to do to become worthy of it. Accepting faith in a satisfaction made on their behalf, is the only way to make removal of sin theoretically comprehensible, but the command that the human being does his duty is unconditional. He must start with improving his life as the supreme condition under which alone a saving faith can occur.

It is sometimes said the first principle leads to ritual superstition, which can reconcile criminal conduct with religion, whereas the second can result in a belief that combines hostility to revelation with exemplary conduct. Faith in the Son of God refers, in itself, to a moral idea of reason, which is both a guideline and an incentive, and it does not matter whether we start from it as rational faith or the principle of good life-conduct. On the other hand, faith in the God-man is not, as historical faith, the same as accepting the principle of good life-conduct, which must be totally rational. But the true object of the saving faith is not that in the God-man, which can be known through experience, but in the prototype that is to be found in our reason, and this is the same as the principle of good life conduct.

However, if purely historical faith were made the condition of being saved, it would create two conflicting principles of faith. All religions have experienced this clash. Priests bemoan neglect of forms of service, established to reconcile the people with God, while moralists deplore the moral decay, for which they blame easy remission of sins. Religious traditions and observances have served a purpose but, as the human being matures, they become a distraction. The moral predisposition requires that religion be freed of its historical aspects, so that the pure faith of religion can rule over all. This will end the distinction between laity and clergy, as there will be equality, due to the freedom which results from each individual obeying the law he prescribes for himself, through reason. God will bring all human beings together under a common government, for which the visible Church has prepared them. This transition to the new order will happen through gradual reform, resulting from the permanent revelation of the principle of the pure religion of reason that is occurring in all human beings. And the kingdom of God can be said to have come into human beings, even if just the principle of the transition from ecclesiastical faith to the universal religion of reason has publicly taken root. Unobserved, the good principle creates its kingdom in human beings, leading to the conquest of evil and eternal peace.

Division 2 (pp. 129–39)

Being based on pure moral faith, religion is not a public matter, so people can only become aware of progress in faith for themselves. When ecclesiastical faith accepts the need to conform to the pure moral faith, the Church universal starts to become an ethical state of God. This is a story of conflict between the historical faith of divine service and that of moral religion, which needs to focus on the part of humanity that recognizes the difference between rational and historical faith, and so will be limited to the Christian Church. Although Judaism immediately preceded it, the latter is not a religion, but a union of members of a certain race under purely political laws. Even those accompanying the ten commandments were coercive, making no claim on the moral disposition. Further, faith in a future life is absent from Judaism, indicating the intention to create a political, not an ethical, community. Christianity was a religious revolution, and was only linked to Judaism as the best means of promoting it. Jesus declared that only moral faith, which proves its genuineness in good life-conduct, can make human beings holy. After giving an example that conformed to the model of a humanity well-pleasing to God, he was shown returning to heaven, though able to assure his disciples he would still be with them, even to the end of the world. Miracles attest to this teaching but, as it is part of a moral and soul-saving faith, are not required. While the pure faith of reason is its own proof, every historical faith needs educated followers to record it, and ensure its continuation. Christianity's early history is obscure, and we do not know if its first followers improved morally.

However, from the time the Romans became interested in it, there is little evidence of the beneficial effect a moral religion should have, but plenty of evidence of superstition, division and persecution. But its true purpose, to introduce a pure religious faith, shines through all this. The problem was that, due to the bad tendencies of human nature, what should have served to win over to this pure faith the nation that was used to its old historical faith became the foundation of a universal world-religion. The present is the best period of church history. The seed of true religious faith, now being sown in Christianity, needs only to be allowed to grow for the visible evidence of God's invisible kingdom on earth to begin to appear, while claims made for revelation are now more modest. What we must do is use the Bible for instruction in church, but not compel people to have faith in it. Further, its purpose is to give a vivid presentation of virtue striving towards holiness, so it must always be used in the interests of morality. The emphasis must be on true religion not being about what God has done for our salvation, but about what we must do to become worthy of it. Governments must not interfere in church matters, as they may hinder the advance in goodness. The kingdom of heaven can be interpreted as a visible one on earth, when those in rebellion against God are defeated, but Jesus' teaching about it was from the moral side: about being citizens of a divine state. He told his disciples what they must do, not just to achieve this for themselves, but to bring others into it. However, he warned them to expect troubles on earth, not happiness, and that their reward would be in heaven. The Church's teaching about its final destiny shows it as ultimately triumphant, with separation of the good from the evil, and victory over its enemies, as the final result of establishing the divine state. All earthly life ends, as death is destroyed, and immortality, involving salvation for one side and damnation for the other, begins. This is a beautiful picture of an age when everyone obeys the moral law, which introducing true universal religion will achieve, and which only faith can foresee as completed. But it does tell us always to be ready for it: to think of ourselves as the chosen citizens of a divine, ethical state, as the kingdom of God is within us.

General Remark (pp. 140–7)

Enquiry into religion always encounters underlying mysteries. Their existence cannot be determined *a priori* and objectively; we have to search our moral predisposition, to see if any exist in us. Doing so will not give us access to the grounds of morality, but freedom, which the unconditional moral law discloses to human beings, through their having the power of choice, is not a mystery, and it is applying it to realization of the final moral end that leads us to holy mysteries. Alone, human beings cannot realize the idea of the supreme good, bound up with the moral disposition, as it relates either to happiness, or to the union of human beings, required to achieve that end. But, as they feel a duty to further it, they feel compelled to believe in a moral ruler of the world, who can make the end possible. Although we must think of God as omnipotent, so he can execute his will, our concern is not with his nature, but his relationship to us as moral beings. Our practical reason demands faith in him as holy lawgiver, benevolent ruler and just judge. There is no mystery in this faith, which states God's moral bearing towards the human race. But, as this purification of the moral relationship between

God and human beings was first made public in Christian teaching, it can be described as a revelation to human beings of something that was a mystery to them, through their own fault. The revelation tells us that, as lawgiver, God is neither indulgent, nor despotic, but concerned with human beings' holiness; that his goodness is his attending first to their moral makeup, by which they can become well-pleasing to him, and only then to their inability to do so, unaided; and that his justice is his limiting his generosity to the condition that human beings abide by the moral law, as far as they can measure up to it. In relation to this set of beliefs, which embody the whole of pure moral religion, it is helpful to think of the one God as, morally, three different personalities. But thinking of the Trinity as what God is in himself is beyond human understanding, and does not aid moral improvement. Reason reveals three mysteries.

(1) Our call to be citizens of an ethical state: we can think of ourselves as subject to divine law only as God's creatures, but this suggests we are not free. We have to think of ourselves as already existing free beings, not as a result of creation, but through moral necessity, which is only possible according to laws of freedom. (2) The mystery of satisfaction: human beings are corrupted, but if God's goodness has called us to be members of the kingdom of heaven, he must be able to make up for our inadequacy from his holiness. But reason demands that the necessary goodness comes from us; that no one can stand in for another; and that, if we need to assume such a thing, it can only be for moral purposes. (3) The mystery of election: even if there is such satisfaction, accepting it indicates that we have determined our will towards the good, which we cannot achieve ourselves. However, if God's grace assists only some human beings, and casts off others, this

does not suggest divine justice, and is a complete mystery. God has not revealed to us why there is moral good and evil in the world, or how, if there is always evil in them, good arises in some human beings, but not others. We would not understand it. He has revealed his will to us, through the moral law, but not how free action occurs. But we know all that we need to know: that the moral law calls us to good life conduct, and that the highest goal of our moral perfection, which we can never reach, is to love it.

Part IV (pp. 151–91)

In the world of understanding, a thing is already there, when the causes capable of bringing it fully into being are in place, even if its complete development, in the world of the senses, lies in the future. This applies to the dominion of the good principle. Setting up an ethical community, as a kingdom of God, creates a strong defence against attacks of the evil principle, but human beings can only do so through religion, and in the visible form of a church, of which God is the founder and human beings its officials and members. The pure religion of reason is an invisible Church, whose members do not require officials, as they receive their orders direct from God. A visible Church, based on statutory laws, can only be the true Church, to the degree that it approximates to the pure faith of religion, which will ultimately lead to ecclesiastical faith being discarded. Church officials who disregard this end, and teach that ecclesiastical faith alone can save, give the Church counterfeit service.

First Part (pp. 153–64)

When classified by origin, religion is either natural or revealed but, when classified by capacity for external communication, is either natural or learned. While its being natural is the essential characteristic of a religion that should bind human beings, communicability is an important indicator of its suitability to be a universal religion of humanity. A religion can be natural, yet also revealed, if human beings could have reached it by their reason, but not as quickly. Revelation is then very advantageous, and people can still use reason to convince themselves of its truth. Examination of the New Testament, which is interwoven with ethical teachings and related to reason, will help to explain what revealed religion is in general.

First Section (pp. 155–60) Natural religion (morality, God and immortality) is a pure practical concept of reason, of which we can convince all human beings, and we can also persuade them that its effect is duty. This has the essential qualification of the true church, validity for all human beings, and so needs only teachers, not officials. But, this rational religion cannot achieve universality, unless it takes the form of a visible church; and, to be the founder of such a church, assumes a fact, and not just a concept of pure reason. If someone preached a universal religion of reason, and suggested forms of observance, as means of establishing a church on its principles, we would accept that church as the true universal one.

Jesus teaches that what pleases God is not carrying out church duties, but the moral disposition; that sinful thoughts are as bad as deeds; that these pure dispositions should show themselves in public deeds, which others can imitate, enabling the kingdom of God to grow; and that duties should be done for their own sake. He dismisses any hope that moral goodness will be a heavenly gift, or divine influence will make good a person's lack of moral perfection. He promises that the sacrifices of good moral conduct will be rewarded in a future world, but that acting prudently, to comply with the moral law, is not acting morally. This is a complete religion, which can be conveyed to human beings through their reason, and its possibility, as a prototype, has been demonstrated in an example, without needing to be proved by miracles.

Second Section (pp. 160–4) If there are necessary dogmas of faith that have been revealed, and so cannot be known through reason, but which need to be preserved, they have to be recorded. Christianity is both a rational and a revealed faith. Reason tells us our life conduct can never justify us before God, but that we need to be so justified, and that ecclesiastical observances are no substitute for righteousness. But, where it is based on facts, not reason, Christianity is faith. This is the foundation of the Church, which must be served according to both its historical faith and the moral faith of reason. However, universal human reason must be recognized as the supreme principle: this is true service of the church, under the dominion of the good principle.

As it has many uneducated followers, Christianity needs scholars, to interpret and preserve its doctrine of revelation, but putting revealed faith above the pure religion of reason is counterfeit service of the Church, as it reverses the moral order, and turns what are mere means into things that are commanded unconditionally. Christianity's advantage over Judaism is that its first teacher preached it as a moral, not a statutory, religion, so it stands in the closest proximity to reason, enabling it to be preached without historical scholarship, at all times and to all people. But, to help its spread, the early Christians interwove elements of Judaism with it. These have become part of its essential articles of faith, and have been added to. This causes difficulties, as is the case, if religion is sought, not within us, but from outside.

Second Part (pp. 164–82)

True religion consists only of moral laws, the unconditional necessity of which we discover through reason. Ecclesiastical laws, which our moral judgement deems arbitrary, exist for the sake of a church. It is a delusion to think that faith in them is essential to God's service, as it is a counterfeit one.

1 (pp. 165–6) Anthropomorphism has serious implications for morality. We fashion for ourselves a God who is undemanding in relation to our moral disposition. We think we should do things just to please him. The more useless, and less directed at universal moral improvement, they are, the holier they seem to be. They may not serve God, but he is believed to see good in those who do them. Such people may be too weak to obey his moral commands, but hope to make up for it in this way.

2 (pp. 166–70) Apart from good life-conduct, anything that the human being thinks he can do to become well-pleasing to God is religious delusion and counterfeit service. Reason tells us that, as long as we progress towards conformity with the law, with an attitude of true devotion to duty, we can hope God will supplement what is outside our power, although we will not know how. But there are no limits to counterfeit service (no form of which is better than any another) of God, whereby the individual offers everything to God, except his

moral disposition, hoping it may be accepted instead. The Church calls what human beings can accomplish, through the strength of the principle of virtue, nature, and what God does to make up for our moral deficiency, grace, but we cannot distinguish the effects of the two. The most we can say is that there must be effects of grace, to supplement the imperfection of our striving for virtue.

3 (pp. 170–8) Serving God through faith in statutory articles cannot make a better human being. Only those whose service is the disposition to good life-conduct, embrace the principle that declares them members of the invisible Church. Moral service alone directly pleases God: actions with no intrinsic moral value can be seen as well-pleasing to God, only insofar as they further moral service of him. When priority is given to observing statutory laws, based on revelation, which are said to be necessary, not as a means to the moral disposition, but to become well-pleasing to God directly, and when historical faith is put above good life-conduct, the service of God becomes fetishism.

Priestcraft is the nature of a church where it, and not principles of morality, predominates. Its clergy will claim the exclusive right to interpret God's will, and will deny members any moral freedom. In the end, through its influence over people's minds, it rules the state as well. It is not just the intellectuals who need to grasp this faith, and it might seem that historical faith, with its accessible narratives, is very suitable for the uneducated. However, the moral law has been written in the hearts even of the least educated. This is what leads to faith in God, or certainly to the idea of him as moral lawgiver, and thus to pure religious faith.

Even when a church serves God by aiming at moral religion

and respect for the moral law, the question arises of the sort of instruction it should give its members: whether its main component should be teaching about divine blessedness, or virtue. There is a risk that church education and preaching will give the former priority over the latter. But the second is what matters, and stands on its own, even without the concept of God; the first is only a means. Divine blessedness cannot be the final end of moral effort. It is only a way of reinforcing what makes for a better human being: a virtuous disposition. It does so by offering to this effort the expectation of the final end, which it cannot deliver itself. The idea of virtue fosters a sense of human dignity, and leads to God, who is worthy of adoration, only as a moral lawgiver. The danger of starting with him as world ruler is that this can become slavish subjection to the commands of a despot. The doctrine of atonement follows from our courage to stand on our own feet, and strengthens it, by showing what cannot be altered as wiped out, and opening up the path to new life-conduct. But, if it comes first, the focus on hopelessly trying to undo what has been done, the sense of our inability to do good, and fear of falling back into evil, undermine our courage.

4 (pp. 178–82) Conscience does not usurp the role of reason, and judge actions in relation to the moral law. It is reason judging itself, as to whether it has adequately scrutinized the rightness or wrongness of actions. An inquisitor acts unconscientiously if he destroys a heretic's life for his religious dissent. So do the clergy, if they use their spiritual authority to force others to believe things beyond their understanding, which they cannot be sure of themselves. Too many religious people adopt the security principle in matters of faith, and believe too much rather than too little. The right approach is

to treat religious beliefs that derive from revelation, but which are not at odds with moral principles, as not certainly true or false, but as likely to be saving, only if a person has not made himself morally unworthy. This is true moral safety: safety before conscience.

General Remark (pp. 182–91)

The good human beings can do, according to laws of freedom, without supernatural help, can be described as nature, as distinct from grace. But, as with everything supernatural, to which morality belongs, the extent of grace's effect is hidden. Supernatural intervention in our moral faculty, to satisfy our duty, is a transcendent concept, outside experience. It is problematic, because reason tells us we gain credit only for good conduct, attributable to our own powers: but freedom itself is equally incomprehensible. As we cannot know anything about the operation of grace, or when to expect its assistance, we should not think about it, in case we disable ourselves from using reason, or become inactive, through expecting God to do what we should do ourselves. The idea of a means of grace is self-contradictory: we cannot become worthy of heavenly assistance, except by improving our moral nature, to fit ourselves for divine approval. True service of God lies in the disposition to perform our duties as divine commands, not in actions carried out exclusively for God. However, human beings need to give this invisible service a visible form, and it then comes to be regarded as the actual service.

Four religious practices can foster attention to true service of God: private prayer; church-going; baptism; and communion. But a practice, not performed in a moral spirit, but only to please God, is fetish-faith. Even when humans see that everything depends on moral good, originating in action, they still look for an easy way, and hope God will treat performing the practice as doing the act itself. Hence, the development of certain practices as a means of grace. Three kinds of delusory faith are: faith in miracles; faith in mysteries; and faith in means of grace.

(1) Praying is a superstitious delusion, if regarded as a means of grace. God already knows our wishes, and it discharges none of our duties. Its only value is to stimulate the disposition to life conduct well-pleasing to God. (2) Churchgoing can strengthen people's consciousness of being citizens of a divine state, which is to be represented here on earth, but thinking of it as a means of grace is a delusion. (3) Receiving members into the church is an important event, but is not a holy action that makes a person receptive to divine grace. (4) Communion emphasizes the idea of a moral community, and encourages brotherly love, but seeing it as a means of grace is a delusion.

Generally, priestcraft is the dominion the clergy have gained over church members' minds, by claiming exclusive possession of the means of grace. In relation to God's moral properties of holiness, mercy, and justice, human beings appeal to the second, to avoid complying with the demands of the first. They leave the job of making themselves better human beings to God, while focusing on piety, not virtue. If people believe they possess special effects of faith, virtue can become irksome to them. It is no surprise people are often said not to be improved by religion, and that their supposed inner light seldom shows itself in good works. At present, there is no evidence that the so-called religious elect will outperform those naturally honest human beings whom we depend on in daily affairs, business and need.

Glossary

Absolution from debt. Being set free from the debt of sin by God.

Adam. The story of Adam and Eve is told in Genesis. Although enjoying a perfect relationship with God, Adam, the first man, chose to disobey God.

Animality. The human being's status as a living being.

Anthropological research. Scientific research into the nature of human beings.

Anthropomorphism. Making something (in this case God) human-like, expressing it in human form.

Antinomy of human reason. Paradox or contradiction, in which reason is at odds with itself.

Apodictically certain. That which can be proved, clearly shown to be true.

Apostle. One sent forth to preach the Christian gospel, particularly the twelve disciples, chosen by Jesus. The quotation is from Ephesians 6.12 (Ephesians is traditionally attributed to St Paul, who regarded himself as one of the apostles).

Appropriation. Taking possession of, taking to oneself.

A priori. That which comes before experience, and which holds (or is claimed to hold) irrespective of experience.

Articles of faith. (The central) beliefs/principles of a particular religious faith, which may be written down.

Authentication rests on a document indelibly retained in every soul. The truth of moral religion, which treats moral duties as divine commands, can be established by reason: it does not depend on a historical document.

Benevolent. Wishing to do good. In Christianity, (infinite) benevolence is an attribute of God, who is believed to wish human beings (his creatures) well.

Biblical theology/theologian. Branch of theology concerned with study of the Bible (Old and New Testaments). See also theology below.

Blessedness. Happiness, enjoying God's favour.

Book of Genesis. The first book of the Old Testament, which contains the story of the Fall. See Genesis chapter 3.

Castigations. Here, self-inflicted chastisement/punishment, designed to please God.

Categorical imperative. The imperative of morality, which commands unconditionally. What it commands must be done for its own sake, and because it is right, not to accomplish some further purpose, so it may conflict with a person's inclinations. In *The Groundwork of the Metaphysics of Morals*, Kant gives five different formulations of the categorical imperative, the first of which is: 'act only in accordance with that maxim through which you can at the same time will that it become a universal law.'

Censorship. State or religious control (and possibly suppression) of what can be published. Kant urges religious censors to consider the interests of scholarship, as well as what they perceive to be the best interests of their religion.

Character of his species. The moral nature of human beings: whether they are good or evil.

Church invisible. The ideal ethical community, in which all morally upright human beings join together under direct divine rule, to serve God by obeying the moral law, and which acts as a model for the actual churches human beings establish.

Church militant. The (combative) Church in the world, engaged in battle with the principle of evil.

Church visible. The actual union of human beings/churches they establish, which (should) approximate, as far as possible, to the ideal of the Church invisible.

Clergy. The ordained ministers of a (Christian) church/denomination (who may be part of a hierarchy from priests to bishops), who lead it. Kant warns that their role as interpreters of its teachings may give them too much influence over church members.

Coercive laws. Laws, imposed and enforced by the state, which people are punished for disobeying.

Cognize/cognizable. Know, knowable.

Communion. The eucharist or mass, which, following Jesus' example at the last supper, is the main act of worship for the majority of Christian Churches. Churches interpret it in different ways. For Kant, it fosters brotherly love, and helps to bind church members together as a moral community.

Glossary

Conscience. Human beings' awareness of what is right or wrong, which deters them from contemplating or performing certain actions. Interpretations of its nature and role have varied. For Kant, it is reason judging itself, as to whether it has adequately scrutinized the rightness or wrongness of actions.

Contradict/contradiction/contradictory. When a proposition and its negation are brought together.

Conversion. (Complete) change of belief or attitude, as when someone who has not believed in God, starts to do so. Kant's concern in *Religion within the Boundaries of Mere Reason* is with transformation of the individual's moral attitude.

Counterfeit service. Bogus service, service that it not genuine: the kind a church is given by leaders who teach that its rules matter more than the pure religion of reason, and obeying the moral law.

Courtly service. The kind of (obsequious and flattering) service/behaviour appropriate in the court of a monarch. Kant thinks religious people tend to turn everything connected with God and their own moral improvement, including prayer, into a form of courtly service.

Creation. The idea that the universe was brought into being by God, rather than coming into existence as the result of natural processes. In Christian theology, God made the universe from nothing.

Creator. Term applied to God as the maker of the universe.

Credentials. Proofs, evidence to support what is claimed to be true.

Creed. Statement of a religion's main beliefs, such as the Apostles', Nicene and Athanasian Creeds in Christianity.

Cult and observances, religion/faith of. One in which acts of worship and devotion play a central part, as it is believed that this, rather than obedience to the moral law, is the service God requires.

Culture. The individual and general human progress that results from interaction with others in society.

Damnation. The condemnation of the wicked, whom God sends to hell.

Debt(s) (of sin). What human beings owe to God as a result of their sins (see below).

Delusion. False belief.

Deontological system of morality. One like Kant's, which treats certain actions as being right or wrong in themselves, irrespective of their consequences. For example, lying is always wrong, even if, in a particular situation, lying would produce more happiness/cause less pain than telling the truth.

Desire(s). What human beings wish to do. They need to overcome their desire(s), in order to obey the moral law.

Determination of the will. Act of willing, deciding what action to perform.

Disjunctive. Limiting the choice to only two possibilities.

Dispensation. Authority, permission.

Disposition. Attitude, inclination, tendency.

Divine. Relating to God; also term for a member of the clergy or someone with expert knowledge of theology.

Doctrine. What is taught, what is believed on the basis of what is taught. Here, religious teaching(s) or belief(s).

Doctrine of atonement. The Christian teaching that, although they have sinned, human beings can be reconciled with God, through Jesus' death and resurrection.

Doctrine of divine blessedness. See grace below.

Doctrine of virtue. Teaching that the way to serve God is to obey the moral law.

Dogma. Belief held on authority, and which may be held, despite lack of supporting evidence, or even evidence that it is not true.

Duty. What all human and rational beings are required to do under the moral law.

Ecclesiastical. Relating to the Church or its clergy.

Ecclesiastical faith. Faith based on revelation; a particular church or religious denomination, whose beliefs, rules and practices are based on revelation. See also statutory laws below.

Ecclesiastical service. See temple service below.

Edification/edify. Improve spiritually or morally.

Effects of Grace. See grace below.

Election. Choice, selection. The idea that God chooses some people for salvation, while reprobating (see below) others.

Empirical. What relates to, is based on, (sense) experience.

Empirical faith. A faith based on, related to experience.

End. That which is desired or aimed at. See also incentive below.

End of the world. See Matthew 28.19–20. After telling them to go forth and 'make disciples of all nations', Jesus assures his disciples that he will be with them 'to the close of the age'.

Enthusiasm. Here, ardent and excessive zeal/eagerness.

Enthusiastic delusion. False belief, arising from enthusiasm: specifically, the belief that there are supersensible means available, by which individuals can make themselves well-pleasing to God.

Eternally/eternal/eternity. Everlasting, forever: in the Christian context, the idea that God transcends time.

Ethical community. Any community/society of people that choose to obey the moral law, and which can exist within the political state that is governed by coercive laws.

Ethical state of nature. When human beings do not obey the moral law for its own sake, but have to be coerced into right conduct.

Ethico-civil state. One in which human beings obey the moral law for its own sake.

Ethics. A term generally used interchangeably with morality. In the *Groundwork of the Metaphysics of Morals*, Kant divides it into an empirical part, practical anthropology, which concerns the application of morality specifically to human beings, and a rational part, morals, which concerns what all rational beings ought to do.

Eve. The first woman, who, according to Genesis 2.22, was created from Adam's rib.

Evil. That which is opposed to good and to God.

Evil being. Satan, an angel who rebelled against God, and tempts human beings to sin. See Genesis chapter 3.

Exegesis. Exposition, interpretation (of the Bible).

Expiation(s). (Trying to) make amends to God for sins.

Exposition. Setting forth, explaining, interpreting (the Bible).

Fact and not just a concept of pure reason. Jesus was an actual human being, who lived, taught and died on the cross, at a certain point in history; he is not just an idea, discovered by the reason.

Faith(s). Kant prefers to use this term to refer to the different ecclesiastical faiths (the various religious groups and denominations), in contrast to religion (see below).

Fall (the). When human beings chose to disobey God, thus ending their perfect relationship with God, and bringing sin and death into the world. See also Adam above.

Father in heaven. God. See Matthew 5.48: 'be perfect, as your heavenly Father is perfect'.

Fear and trembling. See Philippians 2.12.

Fetishism/fetish-service/fetish-faith. The belief that an inanimate object has magical or supernatural powers. For Kant, it is a form of fetishism for human beings to believe that they can please God by performing actions (accepting a church's articles of faith, taking part in its ritual) that lack moral value.

Formal proof. A conclusive demonstration.

Founder of such a church. Jesus, as founder of Christianity/the Christian Church.

Glossary

Freedom. Freedom of the will/free will. For Kant, this is the supreme principle of morality (*Groundwork of the Metaphysics of Morals*). Although part of the world of sense, and subject to laws of nature, human beings, as rational beings, are also part of the world of understanding, and free. Therefore, they are able to subject themselves to moral laws, discovered by their reason, and can be held morally responsible for their actions.

French Revolutionary War. The war (1793–1802) between France and other European countries, following the French Revolution. Hostilities (Napoleonic War) resumed in 1803, and did not end until the final defeat of Napolean at Waterloo in 1815.

Goal of perfection. Complete obedience to the moral law, making it the supreme maxim (see below).

God is all in all. See 1 Corinthians 15.28: 'When all things are subjected to him, then the Son himself will also be subjected to him who put all things under him, that God may be everything to every one.'

God's representative and vicar. Jesus. This refers to teachings about the end of the world and a visible kingdom of God on earth, found in the Book of Revelation (Apocalypse of St John), when Jesus returns and Satan is defeated.

God's Spirit. The Holy Spirit. See Trinity below.

God-man. Jesus.

Golden Age. The period before the Fall.

Grace. In Christian teaching, the help God freely gives to human beings through Jesus Christ.

Ground of its maxims. The basis of its adopting maxims (see below) in accordance with the moral law. The commands of the moral law are unconditional, and must be performed for their own sake, and because they are right, not for any other reason.

Guilt. Culpability, and consciousness of it.

Happiness is proportioned to the observance of duty. See highest good in the world below.

Hate is tantamount to killing. See Matthew 5.22: 'every one who is angry with his brother shall be liable to judgement'.

Heretic. One who holds a religious opinion(s) that is contrary to the accepted teachings of a/his religion/church.

Higher, moral, most holy, and omnipotent being. God, who alone can ensure that obedience of the moral law for its own sake is rewarded with happiness.

Highest good in the world. Although happiness is not the end (see above) of morality, the highest good is obedience to the moral law, for its own sake, being rewarded with happiness. As only God can make this possible, it requires belief in both God and human immortality.

Highest lawgiver. God.

Historical faith. See ecclesiastical faith above.

Holy/holiness. That which is associated with, devoted to, set apart for, God or religion.

Holy law. The moral law, which is the law God commands human beings to obey.

Holy One. Jesus.

Humanity. The human being's status as a living and rational being.

Ideal of holiness. Jesus, who, by embodying moral perfection, is the ideal of holiness.

Idol. False god, image of a god that is worshipped.

Ignominious death. The shameful and painful death Jesus endured, through crucifixion, for the sake of the world.

Illumination. Here, initiates' (see below) false belief that they have (sudden) spiritual insight.

Immortality. Living on after physical death. For Kant, immortality is a postulate of the practical reason (see below): it gives human beings the opportunity to achieve moral perfection.

Incarnation. The Christian teaching that, in Jesus Christ, God became incarnate (took on human nature) to redeem human beings. See also Trinity below.

Incentive. Motive. Morality does not depend on religion: what the moral law commands, not what God decrees, is the only incentive human beings require to recognize or perform a duty.

Inclinations. What human beings like or desire to do, and which they need to overcome, in order to obey the moral law.

Infer. Conclude one thing from something else.

Initiate. One who has recently become a member of (for example) a church.

Innate. Inborn, inherent.

Inquisitor. Here, a religious interrogator/prosecutor, concerned with identifying heretics (see above), and eradicating religious dissent.

Intelligible being. Human beings, as rational beings, belong to the world of understanding, as well as the world of the senses. See also freedom above.

Intelligible (deed). A deed that takes place in the world of understanding, and which, unlike a deed in the world of the senses, is known through reason, not sense experience.

Invocations. Invoking God, calling upon him (to forgive them).

Jesus Christ. (c. 5/6 BC–c. AD 30). Founder of Christianity and the second person of the Trinity (see below).

Juridico-civil. The political state, whose citizens are subject to coercive laws (see above).

Justification. The Christian teaching (of which there are different interpretations) of being/being put in a right relationship with God.

King Frederick William II of Prussia (1744–97). He succeeded his uncle Frederick II (Frederick the Great) as king of Prussia in 1786. During his reign, religious and other forms of censorship were enforced in Prussia.

Kingdom of Evil. The kingdom Satan was able to establish in the world, as a result of the Fall (see above).

Kingdom of God. See Matthew 6.33: 'But seek first his kingdom and his righteousness.' Jesus preached the coming of the kingdom of God, and the idea has been interpreted in different ways. For Kant, seeking the kingdom of God is progress towards conformity with the moral law. See also God's representative and vicar on earth.

Kingdom of Heaven. See Kingdom of God above.

Latitudinarian. One who takes a broad or liberal view.

Law(s). The moral law(s).

Laws of nature. Natural laws. As part of the world of the senses, human beings are subject to them but, as members of the world of the understanding, they are free in relation to them.

Learned faith. Religious belief(s), based on biblical scholarship and church teachings, not the moral law, discovered through reason.

Learned religion. See learned faith above.

Love everyone as yourself. See Matthew 22.39: 'You shall love your neighbour as yourself.'

Love of God. See Matthew 22.37–8: 'You shall love the Lord your God with all your heart, and with all your soul, and with all your mind. This is the great and first commandment.'

Malice. Active ill-will, desire to do wrong.

Matter of indifference to reason. An issue in which reason has no interest.

Maxim(s). A subjective principle or rule of conduct.

Maxim of holiness of disposition. An attitude of performing moral duties/treating them as divine commands.

Glossary

Means of Grace. Kant dismisses the idea that any religious practices, such as sacraments, are means of grace. See also grace above.

Merit. State of deserving well, as a result of good deeds, which God will reward.

Messiah. One anointed or chosen by God, who would defeat Israel's enemies, and restore the kingdom of Israel. In the Gospels, the term is applied to Jesus.

Miracle. Remarkable event, which defies scientific explanation, event attributed to supernatural cause(s).

Model. Jesus, as an example of unconditional obedience to the moral law.

Moral evil(s). Human actions that cause suffering, such as violence, torture and theft.

Moral guide. The moral law.

Moral happiness. A constant disposition towards advancing in goodness.

Moral law(s). The *a priori* moral principles, discovered by the reason, which should govern the actions of all rational beings.

Moral philosophers. Philosophers concerned with moral issues and the general principles of morality.

Moral religion. One, such as Christianity, which treats moral duties as divine commands, and emphasizes good life conduct. See also pure religion of reason below.

Moral world-epoch. An age in which everybody in the world obeys the moral law.

Moral worth. Actions (and, therefore, human beings) have moral worth or value, only to the extent that they are done from duty, not inclination or self-interest.

Moralist. One who enquires into, teaches or practises morality.

Morality. Here, the moral law; generally, system of moral principles, (principles concerning) what is right and wrong.

Morally-legislative reason. Reason, which is the source of the moral law, by which human beings should conduct their lives.

Mosaic law. Law of Moses or Torah, found in the Pentateuch, the first five books of the Old Testament.

Multiform personality. See Trinity below.

Mysteries. Aspects of a religion that cannot be understood or explained scientifically.

Mystical cover. Supernatural form of the narrative.

Natural religion. Generally, what human beings can find out about God, through the use of their reason and from experience, without the aid of revelation. For Kant, this is morality, God's existence and immortality. He also defines it as knowing something is a duty before recognizing it as a divine command. See also highest good in the world above.

Naturalistic unbelief. Unwillingness to accept that there are revealed religious truths.

Necessary consequence. Something that must follow from, be the result of, something else.

Noumenal. See world of the understanding below.

Omnipotent. In Christian teaching, God's power is infinite or unlimited, so he is omnipotent.

Only-begotten Son, without whom nothing that is made would exist. Jesus. See John 1.3 and Trinity below.

Original sin. The Christian teaching that human nature was damaged by the fall, and that human beings inherit a tendency to sin.

Orthodoxy. Here, a church's claim that what it teaches is correct, and must be accepted by its members.

Outer experience. Ordinary experience, sense experience.

Paraclete. Holy Spirit. See Trinity below.

Paul, Saint (believed to have died AD 64–8). Christian missionary and theologian, who preached Christianity to the Gentiles (non-Jews), and whose epistles or letters are part of the New Testament. The quotation is from Romans 3.10.

Penances. A punishment, imposed by a church, or self-imposed, to show sorrow for sin.

Perfectly holy will. A will wholly dedicated to God's service, or completely obedient to the moral law.

Personality. The human being's status as a rational being, who is responsible for his actions.

Personify. Seeing an individual human being as representing, or embodying, a particular idea.

Perversity. Wilfully choosing the wrong course, and/or obstinately pursuing it.

Phenomenal. See world of the senses below.

Philosopher. One who studies and practises/teaches philosophy: the study of ultimate reality, what really exists, the most general principles of things.

Philosophical theology/theologian. Application of philosophical methods to religious concepts, beliefs and arguments.

Physical evil(s). Evil arising from natural features of the world that cause suffering, such as diseases, hurricanes and floods.

Glossary

Physical happiness. Happiness. See highest good in the world above.

Piety. Devout performance of religious duties and ceremonies.

Pilgrimage. Journey to holy place/place of religious importance, or one undertaken for religious reasons.

Politico-civil state. One with a government, and which is subject to the rule of law.

Polytheism. Belief in many gods.

Postulate(s) of the practical reason. That which needs to be assumed, in order to make sense of morality/what we ought to do. According to Kant (*Critique of Practical Reason*), there are three such postulates: God, freedom and immortality.

Power of choice. See freedom above.

Practical reason. Reason when it is investigating or considering matters of morality.

Precept. Maxim, command.

Predisposition. Inclination, tendency towards.

Prefiguration. Sign of something to come.

Priestcraft. Fetish-service (see above) of God, or where a church gives this priority.

Prince of this world. Satan.

Probabilism. Here, what is most likely to be right.

Proceeds from God's being. Of one being with God. See Trinity below.

Propensity. Tendency, inclination.

Proposition. Statement, which may or may not be true.

Protestants. Christians who 'protested' against the Roman Catholic Church; those who are members of Christian churches established after the Reformation.

Prototype. First or original example of something.

Pure rationalist. One who accepts the existence of revelation, but not that it is necessary for religion.

Pure religion of reason. One that recognizes that obedience to the moral law and good life-conduct are the only service God requires, and the only way to become well-pleasing to him, and which treats moral duties as divine commands.

Pure religious faith. See Pure religion of reason above.

Radical evil. Fundamental evil: the presence of a principle of evil in human nature.

Rational being. Any being possessing reason. The moral law applies to all rational beings, not just to human beings.

Rational faith. Faith based on reason.

Glossary

Rationalist. Kant defines a rationalist as one who believes that only natural religion is morally necessary. Generally, one who believes that reason, rather than (sense) experience, is the principal source of knowledge.

Reason. The rational capacity, the ability to reason, possessed by human beings, and which (Kant holds) enables them (and all rational beings) to be free, because they can conduct their lives according to *a priori* moral principles of the reason, instead of being governed by desires and inclinations.

Reason legislating unconditionally. See reason above and unconditional below.

Reciprocal love. Mutual love between human beings.

Redemption. The belief that Jesus' life and death set human beings free from the debt of sin.

Reflective faith. Theological speculation, which cannot yield knowledge.

Religion. In contrast to the many faiths (see above), there is only one true religion: moral religion, the pure religion of reason.

Religion/faith of divine service. See cult and observances, religion/faith of above.

Religion of mere cult. See cult and observances above.

Religious enthusiasm. The false belief that human beings can justify themselves before God, through supposed contact with him.

Religious superstition. The false belief that human beings can justify themselves before God, through acts of religious worship and religious ceremonies.

Reprobate. Cast off, deny salvation to.

Revealed faith. Faith based on revelation.

Revealed religion. Kant defines this as needing to know something is a divine command before recognizing it as a duty. Generally, religion based on revelation.

Revelation. What (it is believed) God has chosen to disclose of himself through, for example, holy scripture and prophets.

Rigorist. One who takes a strict, narrow view.

Ritual superstition. Superstitious belief that taking part in religious ceremonies is genuine service of God.

Rousseau Jean-Jacques (1712–78). Swiss philosopher and author of *Émile, or Education* and *The Social Contract*.

Sacrament. Religious ceremony, such as baptism or the eucharist, which is regarded as an outward sign of inward grace.

Salvation. Being saved. In traditional Christian teaching, God inter-

Glossary

vening, through Jesus, to save/redeem human beings, despite their disobedience and sin, and giving them eternal life with him.

Salvific. Saving.

Satan. Angel who rebelled against God. See evil being above.

Sciences. Here, intellectual enquiry and research.

Sectarian schisms. Factional splits and divisions (within a church).

Self-incurred. Self-imposed.

Seneca, Lucius Annaeus (4 BC–AD 65). Roman politician, Stoic philosopher and author of the *Epistolae Morales*.

Senses. See world of the senses below.

Sensuous. That which relates to the senses.

Sin. Generally, disobeying the law of God. Here, transgressing the moral law, obedience to which is commanded by God.

Son of God. Jesus. See also Trinity below.

Sorcery. Magical arts. See also fetishism above.

Soul. In Christianity, the spiritual element within human beings, which is the seat of personality and individual identity, which lives on after death, and which will be reunited with its body at the general resurrection.

State of nature. The state of human beings before the start of civilization.

Statutory. That which relates to law, and is obligatory or required.

Statutory faith. See statutory laws below and ecclesiastical faith above.

Statutory laws. Laws which people are obliged to obey: in this case the rules, derived from revelation, with which church members are required to comply.

Stoics. School of Greek philosophy, which taught self-control and uncomplaining fortitude in the face of pain and adversity.

Sublime. Awe-inspiring, uplifting.

Supernatural. What is beyond or outside nature, divine.

Supernaturalist. For Kant, one who holds that revelation is necessary to religion.

Supersensible. That which is beyond/transcends the ordinary physical world that we know about through experience/the senses.

Superstition. Belief or practice not based on reason or experience.

Superstitious delusion. The false belief that human beings can become well-pleasing to God without becoming good.

Supramundane. Above this world, supernatural.

Supreme good. See highest good in the world above.

Supreme justice. The justice of God.

Supreme maxim. The moral law and obedience to it.

Glossary

Surrogate. Substitute.

Susceptible. Open to, accessible to.

Teacher of the gospel. Jesus.

Temple. Place of worship, where it may be believed that a god lives. Kant distinguishes between 'temple service', which may have involved worship of idols and sacrifices to them, and 'ecclesiastical service', which involves a religious community worshipping together.

Temporal conditions. Of time, and related to the world of the senses.

Ten commandments. The basic laws of Judaism. See Exodus 20.2–17.

Thaumaturgy. Performing of miracles.

The kingdom of God is within you. See Luke 17.21.

Theocracy. State governed by God directly, or indirectly through his representatives.

Theologian. One who studies and practises/teaches theology.

Theology. Setting out the beliefs and teachings of a religion in a systematic way; academic discipline concerned with the study of religion/religious beliefs and teachings.

Theoretical reason. Pure, as opposed to practical reason. See reason and practical reason above.

Transcendent concept. An idea which is above or apart from the empirical world, one which relates to God.

Trinity. In Christianity, God is believed to exist in three co-equal persons, Father, Son and Holy Spirit (Ghost): the Trinity. God's unity is preserved, by holding that the three persons are of one substance (of one being), so God is three in one. But the teaching has been the subject of intense theological debate over the centuries. It is possible to think of the Trinity in terms of three modes of existence: God the Father: the creator; God the Son: Jesus, the redeemer; and the Holy Spirit: the inspirer and sustainer of Christians and the Christian Church. Kant maintains that it is helpful to think of God's moral relation to human beings in three different ways, but not that this is what he is in himself, as people cannot understand it, and it does not aid their moral improvement.

True human being. Jesus, who was truly a human being.

Ultimate end. God ensuring that obedience to the moral law, for its own sake, is rewarded with happiness.

Unconditional laws. Moral laws command unconditionally: they have no condition attached to them, and do not depend for their fulfilment on anything else.

Glossary

Universal. Moral laws apply universally to all rational beings: a rational being ought never to act except in such a way that he could also will that his maxim become a universal law (*Groundwork of the Metaphysics of Morals*).

Universality. A characteristic of the true church visible, which is aiming at an ethical union of everyone in the world, and in which there is no place for internal divisions.

Vicarious substitute/satisfaction. Person or thing, who undergoes something/makes payment on behalf of another/others.

Virtue. Goodness, moral excellence. Kant describes it as 'habitual compliance with duty'.

Will. The capability of wishing for something and using one's mental powers to try to accomplish it.

Witness to our spirit. See Romans 8.16: 'it is the Spirit himself bearing witness with our spirit that we are children of God'.

World of the senses. Kant distinguishes between the phenomenal world or world of the senses, the world as it appears to human beings, due to the way they experience it, and the noumenal world, things as they are in themselves, which they cannot experience, because of the kind of beings they are.

World of the understanding. The noumenal or intellectual world (things as they are in themselves), as opposed to the world of the senses/phenomenal world (things as they appear to us). As rational beings, human beings belong to the world of understanding, as well as to the world of the senses.